Folklore
and

Folklore and Food

Schiffer Publishing Ltd®

4880 Lower Valley Road • Atglen, PA 19310

Theresa Bane &
Cynthia Moore Brown

Artwork by T. Glenn Bane

Dedication

This book is to thank all the wonderful cooks who have made my life bountiful with delicious, lovingly made home cooking. For our next generation, too, so they will keep the blessings going!

~ *Cynthia Moore Brown* ~

To my little brothers, Vincent and Joseph. I sincerely hope that by dedicating this book to each of you that it makes up for the Big Jim action figure I broke and the whole "Saturn Police" ordeal.

~ *Theresa Bane* ~

Contents

Foreword

Reading the first chapter of Cynthia's book, I was captivated by the tall story this turned out to be. What a refreshing slant on life! She makes you see that what might look like a bad situation can actually turn out pretty good when family and "friends" pull together to resolve the problem. This is the essence of what this book is all about: family, memories, and good food from the kitchen.

If someone were to ask me to recall "kitchen memories," I would have to say the first words that pop into my mind would be both "Mama and Daddy." Growing up in a very structured home, knowing what to expect each day, was a privilege that I do not take for granted. Every weekday my sister, Joan, and I knew that just before our father came home from work, Mama was in the kitchen getting supper ready. Like clockwork my Dad drove up at the same time every evening. She had a big glass of ice water waiting for him as he greeted my sister and me and then proceeded into the kitchen to sit at the built-in booth and visit with our mother. We could hear them laughing and talking about the day.

It was not only that consistent behavior from my parents that gave me a foundation, but also my mother's cooking. Smells from the kitchen ranged from fried chicken to pot roast and fried pork chops. In the winter, my Dad loved a big pot of brown pinto beans cooked with pieces of ham in it. Fried country potatoes, onions, cornbread, and big glasses of milk accompanied this delicacy. My dad liked it so much he would refer to it as "steak" and years later when I was married he would tell me over the phone, "your Mama is fixing steak tonight" and I knew he meant that she had put on a pot of brown beans. I would picture my dad later that night following up with a "snack" and pouring buttermilk over a glass of shredded cornbread that was leftover from the meal.

Food connections to family range not only from the kitchens we grew up in, but also to our extended families. Family reunions bring out the best in women! A woman definitely wants her food to be praised by others, especially if she is in her element in this room of possibilities. I can recall my mother making the best banana cake every year to take to our family reunion. She knew her younger sister's husband just loved it, and daddy liked my Aunt Jewel's cherry pie. No one made better homemade rolls than my Aunt Louise, and that pepper sprinkled in mashed potatoes that I had never experienced before? Well, it was at a farm kitchen table at Aunt Jewel's that I first experienced that delicious change in that white jewel from the earth. I recall my Uncle Pink and Cousin Jessie coming in from the horse barn, stopping to wash their hands and faces in the fresh water that had been carried in from the well. I was both fascinated and amazed by the well pulley as it pulled fresh water up for this family. I lived and grew up in the middle of Oklahoma City in the 1950s and looked forward to me and my sister's bus trip to this small town in the summer to spend a week in this completely distinct environment. However, the consistency of meals, good manners, and time were the same. Thus, this then eight-year-old had no fear at all to be away from her parents. Good food and love were present in this home like my own.

I chose to accept Cynthia's request to write this foreword because we share the same passion. As professional educators, we both know that "once a teacher, always a teacher." Her passion is orally telling stories in the most fantastic expressions that one cannot help but feel you are right there in the moment! I, on the other hand, tend to lean toward writing my stories. As a contributing writer since 2005 for *Greensboro's News & Record*, I feel as Cynthia does, that the past needs to be shared and not forgotten. History is something that should NOT be overlooked. It is the foundation that makes us what we are today, whether it is two hundred years ago, when our ancestors fought in the Revolutionary War in the Battle of Guilford Courthouse, or 2001, when the United States was attacked and became more alert. History can even be what happened in the kitchen sixty years ago or five years ago. These memories in the kitchen are not to be taken lightly. They truly are a part of our lives. The memories are engrained in us, never to be pulled out by any foreign enemy or machine. It is that part of our life that trains us in patience, sharing, caring, and love. It is what we can hold dear to our hearts and even grasp onto when times are hard.

I could go on and on about my own background and mention my mother's beautiful fruit cake, her own homemade rolls, and famous Jello popcorn balls that my own grandchildren continue to make at Christmas with colors of red and green, but I won't. I will let you begin to turn each delicious page and jump into another world of stories and recipes that Cynthia has put together in her own eloquent style. Maybe this will spur you to recollect all those good times you have had in the kitchen with those you have loved.

Etta Skaggs Reid
Professional Educator, Genealogist, & Local Historian
Summerfield, North Carolina

Mabel's Banana Cake Recipe
(Etta's Mama)

Ingredients:

  1/2 cup of shortening
  1 cup of granulated sugar
  1/2 cup of brown sugar
  3 eggs
  1 cup of sour milk (add 1 tablespoon of vinegar or lemon juice to a cup of milk)
  2 cups flour
  1/2 teaspoon of soda
  1-1/2 teaspoons of baking powder
  1/2 teaspoon of salt
  1 cup mashed bananas (sprinkle lemon juice over bananas so they won't turn dark;
      ripe bananas are sweeter)

Directions:

  Preheat oven to 350 degrees
  Flour and grease either two round cake pans or one 9 x 11 inch pan and set aside
  Beat shortening, granulated and brown sugar together with the 3 eggs
  In a separate bowl, sift together the dry ingredients, and then alternate with the
      sour milk
  Mix well and pour in floured and greased pan(s)
  Bake 30 to 35 minutes
  Let cool before icing cake

Banana Cake Icing

Ingredients:

- 2 tablespoons butter
- 1/8 teaspoon salt (dash)
- 2 ounces cream cheese
- 1 box of powdered sugar
- 1 ripe banana, mashed
- 1/2 to 1 cup of chopped pecans

Directions:

Cream together the butter, salt, and cream cheese

Then add the powdered sugar a little bit at a time

Mash 1 ripe banana with a fork

Add the mashed banana alternately with the powdered sugar until you get the right consistency

Stir in 1/2 to 1 cup of chopped pecans, saving a few to sprinkle on top

Pour a glass of milk and enjoy my memory!

Introduction

"Yoo-hoo! Supper's ready," "Come on down," "Dinner's on," and "Come and get it" are just a few old Southern expressions that folks use to call their family to the dinner table to this very day. I am so excited about this particular collection of some of my favorite stories; I have told them for so many years and love each and every one of them like old friends. I hope you will like them too; in fact, I know you will.

All the stories in this book feature food. There are all kinds of wild misadventures involving eating, down-home cooking, getting food, and fun with food. Most of the recipes are Southern favorites. My family recipes are also entwined with Ohio originals brought here when my parents moved to the South. They are from my family, our extended family, the wonderful family I married into, as well as our friends whom we love like family.

We grew up in a Lutheran church with lots of fellowship and the delicious cooking of our members. The cookbooks they compiled and sold over the years are still family favorites twenty-five years later, even with their missing covers and batter-splattered pages. I want to preserve this small part of family history and what better way to do this than with the basic necessity of life — food.

Down South, as they say, the long tradition of cooking, eating, and sharing food with family and friends has not just been practical but social as well. We Southern folks are raised knowing that hospitality is very important. Food and beverages are always offered to your guests at arrival. The culinary specialties and cultures of the other regions of the United States are as interesting as they are varied, but here in the South we have our own unique outlook on the importance of its traditions and family. Like many regions of our great country, Southern family recipes were passed down with love and importance and in trust to keep the family traditions alive. This heritage is as vital to preserving customs and family history as these stories are. In fact, to tell the truth, they go hand-in-hand.

When I began writing, recording, and researching these recipes and stories, I included Mama with her sharp memory and intelligent point of view, and she made me a list of sayings from the South. I told her that this wasn't going to be a book about the South, but I decided that you, dear reader, would be amused with some of the Eastern North Carolina colloquialisms.

Some of my stories are told in a more formal language and cadence. I don't like to do a "fake" Southern drawl, but some of the stories are told in a more relaxed and Southern tonality, and you will see some of these idioms in my stories. Mama made a list of a few of her favorites: y'all (you all); over yonder (over there); tote or carry — such as "I'm gonna carry Mama to the store" (to take something or someone to some place); s'truth (that is the truth); hush your mouth (BE QUIET); and suge, suga; honey; sweetie pie, darlin (all terms of endearment).

What I find also amusing is that Mama has become quite Southern since she's come down here way back in the 1940s. She started cooking more and more Southern favorites with vegetables grown in the gardens of her Southern friends and later those of her boyfriends. Fried okra, collards, and cornbread were on the family table more and more often. My oldest brother and I had gone away to college, so we missed much of the bounty she served. Because of that and my lifelong adult pursuit of dieting, I don't fry or cook some of the true Deep South staples.

Food is a common thread that has run through our folktales for centuries because it is so basic to our daily lives. Once you stop and think about it for a moment, many of our traditional folktales, fairy tales, and personal stories from around the world involve food in some way or another. Didn't we all grow up hearing about how Goldilocks ate the bears' porridge? How the big, bad wolf ate Grandma and then tried to get Little Red Riding Hood as well? What about poor Chicken Licken who had no cultivating help at all?

There's one Turkish folktale in particular that I remembered about a chicken that can gobble down a whole palace room full of jewels. Let us also not forget the fairy tales with forbidden apples, straw for the king's horses to eat that gets spun into gold, and our German friends Hansel and Gretel who were almost on the dinner menu themselves so they pushed that poor elderly lady in the pot to be

the "soup of the day." You see what I mean? These kinds of stories are popular and have been told and retold over the years because they are so familiar.

Families and friends sharing a meal together is a comforting, soft, and warm haven from the cold hard realities of life. In years past, American mothers stayed home keeping house and cooking the family's

Photo by Cynthia Moore Brown.

meals. Yes, it's true, they didn't have our modern and fancy electric kitchens with all the labor-saving appliances we have come to rely on, but they got dinner on the table every night anyway. Cooking back then took long hours to accomplish, so, therefore, it was a source of pride for even "modern" mothers of the 1950s, 1960s, and on into the 1970s. Today we lead busy lives that leave little time for long family dinners of slow-cooked meals around the dining room table. Everybody is on the go all the time, all day long, from sunup to sundown. For families with swim meets, soccer games, dance classes, and the constant lure and bombardment of electronic media, their schedules are hard to keep up with. Family dinners are now eaten in the car on the way to the next activity, meeting, or obligation. Fast-food picked up at the drive-thru is not only common, but has also been made, sadly, necessary.

But, STOP! Take time to give this a priority. The family dinner time is needed now more than ever. The sharing of one another's experiences, talking, and listening to each other is as essential as the sustenance set before them. We need to bond and connect as a family and maintain our relationships with one another. It's so important to put a family meal in the daily schedule too! Families need each other. The heritage of family recipes, and sharing them with one another, is an important way for us to connect.

If you haven't noticed, home-cooking, celebrity chefs, and many cooking shows are very popular on the television, in books, and in the movies. As a result, more men and women are spending quality time in the kitchen cooking for fun and not just to get a meal on the table.

This all being said, now I will go back to the beginning.

One day, after a particularly bleak diet program lunch, I was telling folktales to a library audience. Now maybe it was because I was hungry for some good tasting food or maybe it was because I had watched one too many of those fancy cooking shows that have taken over several channels that draw you in like a zombie (gee, I even record the ones I miss in case there is something profoundly amazing, like an earth-shattering new recipe for cooking chicken in a whole brand new way); but whatever it was, that afternoon I told an hour's worth of folktales that all revolved around food.

Yes, that's right, food. Eating it, growing it, wanting it, eating too much of it, being starved for it, and eating someone else's. I told stories about giving it away, selling it, cooking it, and losing it. Food glorious food! I told the one about the mother who sends her child off to sell the family cow, and the one about the

Photo by Karl Fargo.

mother who needed some baking soda from the store in town for baking biscuits. Yikes!!! I was so hungry by the time I was finished that I just had to stop on the way home from the event for a little snack. I feel now that I can confess to you that it wasn't a diet drink or a low-calorie anything that I ate that day. No, it was a yummy, and good, and deeply satisfying treat.

Needless to say, this whole thing got me to thinking. Many folktales, fairytales, and just plain old stories from anywhere in the world involve food. There were so many that came to mind that I started making a list. I filled up a whole page, and then another one, and another one — and these were only the stories that I knew and told routinely! Who knows how many more are out there?

Now some of you may be thinking that I am obsessed with eating and food in general. Well, yes, I confess, it's true, I am. I eat and diet compulsively. This book is good therapy for that, I suppose...BUT that's not what I want to share with you. The whole family and food connection is the important point, so back to my story...

I began doing a little bit of research to think about this book idea. The idea grew and grew like Jack and his magic beanstalk vine. Some ideas came from the South, some recipes came from my family heritage, and some came from my husband's family. From the massive list I compiled, I chose the ones that were the most entertaining and fun. A few of the stories I selected could be classified as "tall tales." I created some stories while adapting others. You will find ones you grew up with as well as a few you never heard before.

"But wait," you say, "what about all the recipes?" Well, that idea just seemed to be a natural addition to all this talk about eating and cooking. If after reading a story about fluffy, white biscuits you get hungry for some, why, right there at the end of the story is a recipe for the very same biscuits you just read about. How handy is that?

I picked some favorite family recipes that reminded me of happy occasions. My mother and grandmothers were good cooks. My mother made the Ohio specialties that she grew up with, as did both my grandmothers, but after many decades of living in the South, Mama had added Southern cooking to her standard fare. As for me, after forty years with my husband, Fred's, family I have grown to love many of their recipes, so it was only natural that I include them as well. I also like to improvise on recipes and invite you, dear reader, to add your own twist to them after you have tried them the way they are written.

When I began studying the stories included in this book, little memories of the foods from my own personal history came to mind, so like the stories, some of the recipes are old favorites that we're all familiar with. Why? Well, we live in a troubled world and I think that it helps us to cope with the wars, natural disasters, and our other problems when we have a secure and comforting place to retreat to — a world built with strong family values and that is well-grounded by family traditions.

I love history, tradition, and family. My parents, especially my father, raised us kids to believe that family was of the utmost importance. Daddy taught us that we all needed to study history so that we could live life to the fullest in the present. Taking old-time stories, pairing them up with old-time recipes, and sharing them with a whole new generation would make my daddy very proud.

Enjoy the stories as you read them and then cook up some of the good food in the recipes that follow. Perhaps you will be reminded of your own family favorites as well as your family's history and memories. I hope that this little book of ours will be a small part of it all.

1 | SODY SALLYRATUS

A Mountain Tale with a Recipe for Southern Biscuits

Up in the mountains, in the holler, that's where the family lived: Grandma and Grandpa, Pa and Mama, all their young'uns, and a bunch of family pets.

Mama was busy in the kitchen, making ready to bake some biscuits, as she planned on taking them to the Sunday Go-To Meeting after church where they were all going to have a good time. There would be some square dancing and music and, of course, lots and lots of delicious home-cooking.

Mama was known for her biscuits; everyone said hers were best and she was only too happy to make a big batch for the Sunday Go-To Meeting. She got her big blue bowl out and put in the cups of flour, a cup of lard, a pinch of this, and a pinch of that. She reached up to open the cabinet door—C-R-E-E-E-K—to pull out that special white stuff that makes biscuits and cakes puff up so. You know what I'm talking about — baking soda. She got out her can and she shook it into the bowl and... Oh my gracious, Mama was all out of baking soda!

She looked about and grabbed around up there in the cabinet, trying to find some baking powder, but she was all out of that too. Well, this was not good, not good at all! That meant that her biscuits were gonna be flatter than a pancake and that old Iola Smith, why, she was just gonna be teasing Mama up and down something awful, saying that her own sweet potato biscuits were much better than Mama's flat ones.

Well, Mama just got to worrying about that and she said, "I reckon I got to call Pa in from the field and get him to go down the mountain to the store for me."

Now, back then in those days, there weren't big giant shopping stores. Oh no, there weren't any big stores where you could go buy your food. Nope, you raised your food; you got your food from the fields and your own cows and chickens and eggs — and what you didn't raise, your neighbors did. Everyone helped out each other, giving and sharing.

As for Pa, he was down in the lower forty, plowing. No tractors back then so he had long hours of hard work pushing a plow behind a mule. Grandpa was busy working in the house garden. The tomatoes were about to start comin' in and with all the rain they'd gotten, the weeds were trying to take over.

Ma stood on the front porch and hollered out, "Yooooo-hooo!"

Pa heard Mama a-calling and he looked up toward the house and saw her on the porch. He stopped his work and came a-running as fast as he could 'cause now he heard her ringing on the bell that hung there on the porch. When he finally reached her, puffing and panting, he asked, "Is everything all right, honey?"

Mama shook her head and said, "No, everything is not all right. I've run out of baking sody and my biscuits are gonna be flatter than a pancake at the Go-To Meeting after church on Sunday, and you know how that old Iola Smith can be. She's gonna tease me something awful. She's always trying to have the best biscuits. I need you to go down the mountain and into town to buy me some sody so I can make a big batch of biscuits to take."

Pa was not happy; he had run so fast and hard because he had imagined something terrible had happened. He said to Mama shaking his head no, "I have got to get back down there and do that plowing before the day is done. What are ya bothering me for with this, honey? You just need to send somebody else." With that, Pa turned and started walking back to his plow.

"Oh, all right," Mama said to no one in particular as she thought about what Pa had said. "I'll send... hmm, I guess I'll send Grandpa."

So she stood on the front porch and hollered out toward Grandpa, "Yooooo-hooo!"

Grandpa heard Mama calling, and even though he was busy over there in the house garden, he came as quick as he could. It was a busy time of year, don't ya know. When he finally reached Mama, puffing and panting, he said, "Is everything all right?"

Mama shook her head and said, "No, everything is not all right. I've run out of baking sody and my biscuits are gonna be flatter than pancakes at the Go-To Meeting after church on Sunday. I need you to go down the mountain and into town to buy me some sody."

Grandpa shook his head "no" as he spoke. "I have got to get back over there and do that weeding before the day is done. You just need to send somebody else." With that, Grandpa turned and started walking back to the garden to complete his chores.

Now Grandma was quilting on the porch and had overheard everything that was going on and said to Mama before she could even ask, "I can't go down the mountain and into town for ya. I'm busy working on my quilt because we're gonna have a big quilting party. I have got to get ahead and get stuff ready. 'Sides, my arthritis is actin' up today and I got a hitch in my giddy-up." With that, Grandma went back to her quilting.

Well, Mama was just about to give up. She refused to go to church with all those flat, flat, flat biscuits. She decided to call upon her two young'uns who were out and about playing somewhere with their many pets. Who knows where they were, no doubt lollygagging around somewhere. So Mama stood out on the porch and gave them a holler, "Yooooo-hooo!" and they came a-running — and so did all of their pets. They had dogs and they had the cats, rabbits, and squirrels, just all kinds of pets. They all came a-running. Well, except for the family's little flying squirrel. He jumped right off the mantel board where he liked to stay and was just a-chirping and a-squeakin'.

"Well," Mama said, "listen up, you children. I have got to send you all down to the store. Now I don't want you wasting time lollygagging around down there. No hearing stories, no eating anything out of the pickle barrel. I'll let you both get some of that stick candy you like as long as you promise to get back here real fast. Now I know the both of ya are always forgetting what you're going to the store for so I'll fix that." Mama thought for a moment what she could do to help the two young ones remember.

"I could write it down for you, but no, you'll forget I did that. I could put it in your pocket, but no, I'm afraid that you'll lose it."

Suddenly, a brilliant idea came to her. "I'll tell ya what; I'll teach you two a song. You're going for soda. Baking soda. So here's how you remember it: Sody. Sody. Sody Sallyratus. / Sody. Sody. Sody Sallyratus."

The kids started off down the mountain singing the song Mama had just taught them. They sang it all the way down the mountain and around the bend and through the creek and over the river and finally made it to the country store singing, "Sody. Sody. Sody Sallyratus. / Sody. Sody. Sody Sallyratus."

As soon as they got in the store, they got their stick candy, then they heard one or two short stories over by the pickle barrel, and lastly, they got that Sody Sallyratus. They gave the money for it and put the sody in their pockets as they headed on out the door.

They walked out the door, over the river, and rounded the ridge when all of a sudden, out from behind a tree, jumped a mean ole grizzly bear. ROAR! He had those big, big black bear claws and he just took one look at those two delicious morsels and just ate up that little boy...yum yum yum...and then just as quick, he

ate that little girl too...yum, yum, yum... After that, though, 'cause of the sody in their pockets, he was as big as a pine tree and out to here. Tsk, tsk, tsk...

Now back home, Mama was beginning to get a little bit nervous waiting on her two children to come back home. She looked out the window and she didn't see those young ones coming. She stood out on the front porch and she hollered out, "Y'all coming?" She didn't hear nothin.

Inside the house the little flying squirrel was getting a bit hungry. He was racing back and forth on the mantel board saying in squirrel squeaks, "Where's my supper? Where's my supper?"

Mama waited and waited. She wanted someone to go looking for her children for her. Pa was still plowing the lower forty, Grandpa was still working the garden, and Grandma was still quilting. Mama sighed out and said, "I reckon I'm just gonna have to go myself."

So, she took off her apron, petted the little squirrel on the head, and went on down the mountain all by herself.

Sody. Sody. Sody Sallyratus.

She was singing a little bit to herself just 'cause it was fun, but also, it helped her not to worry.

It was a nice spring day and she heard the birds chirping. The wildflowers were blooming with birds flitting around. She walked down the mountain, around the bend, through the creek, and over the river, arriving at the country store.

Well, there was a big gathering over there now. The menfolk were sitting out front in their rocking chairs just a-rocking and a-talking and a-gossiping. I guess you all didn't know that men can gossip more than ladies. Mm-hmm.

Mama went on inside and she had herself a pickle from out of the pickle barrel. She said to the menfolk sitting there, "Has anyone seen my two young ones?"

"Why, yes, they were here earlier," said old man Crothers who took care of the store. "They were right in here and they got that baking sody. I sure am looking forward to those biscuits of yours at the Go-To Meeting after church on Sunday." He flashed Mama a real big toothless grin.

Mama's busy in the kitchen making ready to bake some biscuits as she looks out at her husband, who's busy plowing the field.

Mama said, "Well, I haven't seen them. I looked on the path coming down here and didn't run into them on their way back up the mountain. Anybody know where they are?"

Everybody who was there said, "Why, no. We ain't seen them since they left. You need some help looking for them?"

Mama shook her head and said, "No, no, that's all right. They're probably just lollygagging out on the path like I told them not to, but when I get a hold of both of them, I am gonna jerk a knot in their hair. I'm just so worried 'cause I don't know where those two young ones could be."

Mama kind of stomped off the porch and went down the path out of town, over the river, and around the bend when all of a sudden, out from behind a tree, jumped that mean old grizzly bear. ROAR! He was real big now and he had those mean ugly, black claws out, and he ate pretty Mama up in one bite. Yummy, yummy, yummy...and that bear, he was now bigger than a pine tree and way out to here. Tsk, tsk, tsk.

Meanwhile, back at home, Pa had come in from his work. He was washing his hands and looking for a little bit of something to snack on before dinner. Grandpa was there now, too, with Grandma, and none of them could figure out where Mama and the young'uns were. Well, it was a big mystery to everybody. They drank some lemonade and settled down in the rocking chairs to wait on Mama.

The little squirrel knew, though, didn't he. Mm-hmm. He jumped off the mantel board and didn't even say a chirp or a chip to nobody. He jumped out onto the front porch and headed down the mountain, scampering fast as he could on his little squirrel feet. All the way he sang "Sody. Sody. Sody Sallyratus. / Sody. Sody. Sody Sallyratus" down the mountain, around the bend, through the creek, and over the river, arriving in town and at the country store.

He looked around and didn't see anybody he knew, so he scampered on out the door, off the porch, down the path, over the river, around the bend, and there he came up against the tallest, the furriest mountain he ever had seen, and wouldn't ya know, it was that bear.

That big old bear had his long black claws out and he opened up his great big mouth all ready to swallow that little squirrel up whole. Just then the little squirrel with his little knees just a-knocking — yes 'um, squirrels do so too have knees — decided he had best just try to scare that bear away. He gathered up his courage and said in the biggest voice he could muster, "Boo!"

Well, wouldn't ya know it. Nobody had ever stood up to that bear before, let alone say "boo!" to him, and when he heard that "boo," it scared him so much that he turned tail and started running down the mountain, tripping over this and tripping over that, crashing into trees, just having an awful time. Finally he tripped over a big log and POW! He split wide open when he fell — and out flew the mama, out flew the little boy, out flew the little girl, and they were just fine. The story has a happy ending, my friends. Mama and her two children stood up and brushed themselves off, 'cause now they had that white baking soda everywhere on them. That soda had puffed up like a cloud of snow, and to their amazement the bear was back down to his normal size. He was feeling quite a bit ashamed for showing off how scared he was, so Mama led him right on back home where Grandma stitched him up with her quilting thread. They even kept him as a pet for the longest time.

I tell you what; those were some of the best biscuits that family ever had. They ate and ate and ate them all that night and all the next day with Grandma's molasses and preserves. They all took turns telling each other the story.

Come Sunday after church at the supper, everybody loved Mama's biscuits and Grandma's sweet potato biscuits too. They heard the story of what had happened, and do you know who the star was? The little squirrel, of course. He just sat up there on the top of the rocking chair, pleased and proud as Mama told the story again and again, and every time she told it, she always said at the end, "Well, I'll tell you what, friends, you need to learn a lesson from our little squirrel here. You should try, and then try again, 'cause even though you're little, you can still make a big difference."

Southern Sweet Potato Biscuits

(Yields about 18 Biscuits)

Ingredients

- 2 cups all-purpose flour
- 2 teaspoons baking powder
- 1 tablespoon sugar
- Pinch of salt
- 1 egg, slightly beaten
- 1 cup of sweet potatoes, cooked and mashed
- 1/2 cup of milk

Directions:

- Combine the ingredients in the order given and mix them up adding the flour a little at a time until soft dough is formed
- Turn the dough out onto a lightly floured work surface and shape into a ball; knead 3 or 4 turns, (do not over knead)
- Press out to a flattened circle, 1/2 inch thick
- Dip your biscuit cutter into flour and cut into 2 inch rounds
- Arrange your biscuits with the edges touching on an ungreased or parchment-lined baking sheet.
- Bake in a preheated oven at 450 degrees for 10 or 12 minutes or until they look golden brown.

Angel Biscuits

Ingredients:

- 1 package of dry yeast
- 2 cups of buttermilk
- 5 cups of flour
- 2-3 tablespoons warm water
- 1 tablespoon of baking powder
- 3-5 tablespoons of sugar
- 1 teaspoon of salt
- 1 cup of shortening
- 1 teaspoon baking soda

Directions:

Dissolve yeast in warm water. Sift dry ingredients together. Cut in shortening, stir in yeast mix and buttermilk. Roll out on a floured board, cut with a cutter and brush tops with melted butter.

Bake at 400 degrees until brown. Dough may be kept refrigerated for several days. Gives you lots of biscuits and compliments. Great for sharing!

Notes from Cyn:

A version of this story has been told for decades in the South and especially up in the mountains of North Carolina. Why, you can probably sit on a front porch and still hear it. As for the biscuits, they have made me so hungry, I think we ought to go whip up a batch. Now, my favorite place to get the biscuit flour is, of course, the Old Mill at Guilford near Oak Ridge, North Carolina. I got a recipe with their mix from them just the other day for sweet potato biscuits. So we can make those and regular biscuits, and it will be like we are eating right there with them in the story.

2 | TAILY-PO, TAILY-PO

An Old Tale with a Recipe for Brunswick Stew done Summerfield, North Carolina style

He lived out in the woods by himself and he liked it that way. He had a small log cabin; he didn't go to town for much of anything. If there was something he needed to eat, he grew it in his garden or he went hunting for it in the woods.

As he was a hunting one day, there was nothing anywhere to hunt. Now he loved animals; he had two dogs that he loved more than anything on this here earth. He loved them so much he didn't even get lonely for a wife because he had those two dogs.

Well, as he was hunting, he got tired. Stretching, he thought to himself, "Well I guess tonight I'm gonna have some old leftovers for dinner, there is nothing around." Because the darkness was coming and he didn't like to be deep in the forest by himself during the darkness, he hurried on home.

He and the dogs were heading home when he saw it. Sticking out of a hole in a tree was just a little bit of fur. He thought, "Well, now ya know I could take that fur to make me a fancy hat and eat the rest of it for dinner."

Whose taily-po did this fur belong to?
We might never know…

So he took a hold of the fur and he pulled, but it didn't come out. So he pulled and he pulled and he pulled. He fell back on the ground and he had not a piece of fur, but a long furry tail. He hadn't heard an animal squeal. He hadn't heard anything, he just had a tail.

His first impulse was that he was gonna throw it down on the ground, but just then his stomach started growling and he was getting so hungry. Now I know that you and I wouldn't eat a furry tail, but remember how hungry he was. So he thought to himself, "I'll take it home, strip off the fur, and just boil the meat and use it to give a little flavor to a stew." That is just what he went and did.

He put the tail in his backpack and he and the dogs started on back home. By now the darkness was coming on and as he walked he got a little bit nervous. You ever have that feeling that you are not alone? Well, just then he heard an eerie song being sung, and it is very weird to hear a song in the woods when you are there by yourself and you know that nobody is around for miles and miles. The song went like this: "Taily po, tail po, I wants my taily po."

The man thought to himself, "Oh no, I had better get out of here. Something belongs to this tail." Without even thinking any more about it, he shoved the tail in his backpack and—whoosh—ran all the way home with his dogs chasing after him the whole way. When he got home, he went and slammed the front door—POW! and put a great big cross bar across it and thought to himself, "Whew! That was no song I heard being sung, I was just hearing the wind blow."

Now more relaxed, he went and got his big cooking pot out, poured the water in from the well. He put in a carrot, salt and peppers, tatter, spices, garlic, pepper, and the tail — plop. He started stirring and stirring and stirring some more. He built the fire so it was blazing by now and the dogs were a-sitting close and waiting on the stew because by now it was smelling delicious and they wanted some.

You couldn't even see the tail in there anymore for all those delicious vegetables. Soon it was making him so hungry, but he thought to himself, "I'm gonna let it simmer just a little while longer and then I'm having supper."

Suddenly he stopped... He heard the wind howling again — and he heard what he thought was an eerie song being sung "Taily po, tail po, I wants my taily po."

He thought to himself, "I'm just hearing things. I'm tired. I'm hungry." So he ladled out some soup, very careful not to get the tail in his bowl. He gave some to the dogs, but he gave himself a great big bowl. He was just beginning to eat it when the wind started blowing even harder than before, and that's when he heard the eerie song sung even louder "Taily po, tail po, I wants my taily po."

This time, before he could say a word of reassurance to himself, he felt the whole house shake — rumble, rumble, rumble — and before he could say another word or think another thought he heard heavy tromping feet — tromp, tromp, tromp. The dogs started barking — woof, woof, woof. He was so scared by now that he was shivering and he thought, "I think I'm gonna go to bed early."

He banked the fire and he got into bed. He pulled the quilt up over his head and called the dogs up into the bed with him. In no time at all he figured that he would drift off to sleep, but he didn't. He couldn't fall asleep because the wind was blowing even harder now and once again he heard the eerie song of the woods even louder than before "Taily po, tail po, I wants my taily po."

It was then he heard at the door "scratch, scratch, scratch" followed by a loud BANG. That cabin door blew in right onto the floor despite having been locked with a heavy crossbar. He sat straight up in the bed and heard those horrible words whispered in an angry whisper "Taily po, tail po, I wants my taily po" and in the darkness he heard something say "GOT IT!"

To this day, sometimes somebody walking in the forest might hear eerie echoes of "taily po, tail po, I gots my taily po."

Southern Brunswick Stew

(Yields about two gallons)

Ingredients:

2 to 2-1/2 pound hen boiled and deboned
1 pound of beef
1 pound of pork
3 cans of diced tomatoes
1 can of cream corn
2 cans of whole kernel corn
4 or 5 potatoes, quartered
1 large onion, chopped
1 to 2 large cans of tomato sauce
2 teaspoon of Texas Pete or Tabasco sauce
Chicken stock as liquid is needed
Salt, pepper, garlic to taste

Directions:

You'll want to cook this in an extra large pot. A cast iron pot may be used if you plan
to cook over an open fire; if you do, double the recipe for a large pot and make
sure you cook it for half an hour longer.
Cook the pork and beef till fork tender then add all the other ingredients
Cook slowly for 2 to 2-1/2 hours; stir frequently
Add the chicken stock whenever the stew gets too thick then add seasonings to taste
This freezes well.

Notes from Cyn:

I have heard various versions of this old folktale including one from Ireland that has
a cute song and a different twist for the ending. Some sort of Brunswick stew has been
cooked with fall or harvest celebrations in the South for decades, maybe even longer! This
recipe I've included here is a modern one. In the "olden days" any kind of meat or game that
had been caught while hunting was used in place of the beef and pork. Fresh vegetables
were used and the varieties varied with the harvest. The stew was usually cooked in a big,
black, cast iron pot, over an open fire with lots of fellowship, music, and storytelling during
the cooking. Once again, food is the center of family and friends' lives. Around here and
across North Carolina many churches, volunteer fire departments, and other groups cook
massive amounts of Brunswick stew to sell as a money maker.

3 | I'M NOT READY TO GO

A Tale of Devotion with a Recipe for Hummingbird Cake

The first birds of spring came as they always did, tweeting and singing their songs. It served as a gentle reminder to the kindly man, letting him know that spring was not far behind all those long cold winter days that he had just suffered through. It had been a particularly bad winter that year with lots and lots of snow. The man, having such a big and gentle heart, had to feed his bird and animal friends even more than usual because of the weather. His own food stores had even gotten dangerously low. His garden didn't provide as much as it used to and this time his food almost didn't last throughout the whole of winter. All he had to do was somehow manage and wait till spring.

The goldfinches came first and frequent, with their dull golden colors made dreary by the winter months. Our friend couldn't wait until he saw their little feathers turning bright and shiny and glowing golden once again. All he had to do was wait till spring.

He went outside each day and would hold out a handful of birdseed. Astonishingly enough, the birds had no fear of him as they knew him to be kind and gentle. They would land on his hands and eat the food he so graciously offered. He ate his own breakfast outside with the birds and the gentle animals. He ate his lunch outside with the birds, too. Although he lived alone, he was never lonely because he had his bird and animal friends to keep him company.

At last spring had come. Summer followed, but all too soon fall's colors were making the forest and gardens beautiful. One day, late in the season, he was outside enjoying the azaleas and the flowers and the crisp fall air when he happened to look down the road. He saw that a stranger was coming. The man had lived here his whole life and had known everybody from around these parts. Even after his wife had passed away all those years ago, he had not considered moving from his little cottage, leaving his friends, the animals, and especially the birds.

The stranger drew closer and closer. He was dressed in black, from head to toe. For some reason the man felt that the stranger was radiating some sort of ominous and sinister feeling. Finally the stranger reached the gate and there he stopped. He didn't come into the garden, but he spoke in a deep and powerful voice "I've come. It's your time. Death is at your gate."

Well, it took more than a moment for that to sink in with our friend, the man. Finally he was able to comprehend what had been told to him and he exclaimed in fear and awe and some bit of anger "It can't be time for me to go yet, I am young.

I am only sixty years old. You are wrong, you have the wrong person. Go away."

Death was so taken aback by someone answering, especially in the tone that the man had used, that he did as he was told. Death turned away and left.

However, the next morning as our friend, the man, was out feeding his birds and enjoying his cup of tea while watching the goldfinches flitter and fly about he saw the black and ominous figure coming down the road again. This time Death seemed taller and even more menacing than he did just the day before. When Death reached the garden gate, this time he leaned down and opened it up and stepped inside. When he spoke, his tone was even more threatening than the man remembered it being. Death said "I told you, I have come for you. I have your name right here in my book."

The man studied Death, but did not see him holding anything at all, let alone a book. That did not really matter, though. The man was truly worried. "Please, please," he began, "I can't leave now. If I leave who will feed my birds? Fall is here now, but winter will soon be upon us. And that's when they really need to have me here the most. Why, the birds are like my family."

Death was not impressed, but he could not argue logic with the man. He bellowed out "That's ridiculous!" He then turned and marched right out of the garden and back up the road from whence he came.

The rest of Fall passed without another visit from Death. The leaves fell and the gardens were beginning to become bleak. The man enjoyed each and every day with his friends, the birds. Those were truly blessed times.

The air became crisp and then colder and colder. All too soon the frigid winds and snow were beginning to come. There was a feeling in the wind that troubled our friend, the man. Then one morning, the ominous figure appeared on the road yet again. It was Death.

"Oh no," the man thought, "what am I going to do? I have to think of something that will get me through this winter so I can take care of my dear friends. If I can just get him to wait till Spring."

Death walked down the road and right up to the garden gate. He opened the gate and stepped inside, walking up to the man who stood on the front porch. As he did so, the man was already talking, trying to explain to Death all the possible reasons why he should not be taken away this time.

Finally Death just shook his head; you could not even see his face, as it was so dark and shadowed even in the bright fall sunlight. With a heavy sigh Death said, "Alright. I don't usually do this, but if you can answer me a riddle, I will give you a little more time."

Death comes a-calling, but, with the help
of his beloved birds, our gentleman friend
is able to stave him off.

The man could not be happier for this chance. The birds and animals were counting on him for their survival.

Death said, "What first walks on four legs in the morning, then on two legs in the afternoon, and finally on three legs in the evening?"

When death spoke the riddle, the man smiled, as he had heard this riddle many times before as it was an old one. He already knew the answer. The man laughed and said, "Oh Death, everybody knows that! You crawl when you're a baby, that's walking on four legs. You walk when you are a man, that's walking on two legs. And then you use a cane when you grow old and become elderly, that's walking on three legs."

Well, Death was upset with how fast our friend had answered the riddle and said in a much darker tone "Alright then, I have a riddle that you will not be able to solve. What's the first thing that your father said on the day that you were born?"

The man stopped and he thought and he finally said, "That's ridiculous, how can I possibly know what my father said the day I was born?"

Feeling most triumphant, Death declared, "Then you are ready to go, come with me!"

"No!" said the man. "No, just let me think about it. Give me overnight. Come back in the morning." The old man could already feel the chill of the air growing colder and colder all around him. He knew that if he was not here this winter there would be no one to feed the birds and his animal family.

Death did not say a word. Instead he stomped off in a foul mood. However, the evil and sinister feelings he came with didn't leave with him, they seemed to stay behind in the garden with a deeply frightening feeling.

Our friend went into his house and fixed himself a meager meal of some porridge and bread. He fed his animal friends and then sat down beside his fireplace, trying to think what his father would have said on the morning of his birth. His father was a good man and his parents had been good to him. They were a big family with ten children who all worked the farm. Most of them were still alive, but of the few who had passed, they had lived on to a ripe old age. That was another reason the man could not figure out why Death was here so early for him. He was only sixty — and sixty was not old.

"Arrg," he thought, "I will never know the answer to this."

That night, he put a whole lot of extra food and seeds and everything that he had been collecting all summer out in bins and troughs. It was a wide array of food for his little furry and feathered friends.

He said a tearful goodbye to each of his little friends. It was as if the charm of the goldfinches knew something was wrong, for they were tweeting wildly. Of course, the mocking birds were always complaining, and though it was too late for them to be around, he imagined that he could hear the drum of hummingbirds' wings as they zipped around the garden as fast as ever sipping up as much nectar as they could.

Our friend blew out all of his candles, closed all the drapes, and laid down on his bed to wait for Death. Oh, if only this could wait till spring! He was feeling so very tired. He was weary to his very bones and could hardly stay awake. He went to sleep before darkness had even fallen.

The next morning when he awoke at dawn he was so stiff and tired he could not get out of bed. Death was not there yet. "Oh, maybe he's not going to come," our friend, the man, thought hopefully. However, as he lay there, he heard the squeak of the garden gate "CREEEEK" and he knew that Death was here for him. He also knew that he had no answer for the riddle that was put to him.

Just then the man heard the birds outside his window. He had always opened his window in the morning, it was the first thing he did every day. He did it so that he could listen to their songs as he busied himself in the house as he made his own breakfast each day. This morning was different. Death was coming for him, he felt so weak and so tired and so old that he could barely push open the shutters.

A whole flock of birds descended down from the sky and landed on his windowsill. It was not just his precious little goldfinches, hummingbirds, and cardinals, but also blue birds, chickadees, mockingbirds, robins, orioles, woodpeckers, and wrens. They were all tweeting and chirping at once. It was a wonderful cacophony of noise, but to the old man, it sounded like he was listening to something important, but he could not tell what as he had been getting hard of hearing. What he did make out was the footsteps of Death as he approached.

"Oh, no!" he thought. "Death is coming, he's at the door." He didn't even knock; Death just swung the door open silently. He stood there for a moment in the doorway, tall and menacing.

The birds did not fly away like they usually would have if a stranger had opened the door and startled them. Instead they were still chirping and chirping and it was as if they were desperately trying to talk to the man.

Our friend was used to this, as the birds would chirp to him often, but amongst it all he heard one little goldfinch's voice and it sounded like he was saying something. Our friend tore his eyes away from Death for just a moment and concentrated with his last ounce of strength. The man was able to figure out what the little goldfinch was saying, "Open the window."

"Open the window." That is what the old man thought he heard the golden little bird saying to him. That was silly, birds don't talk, but as he turned his head about to take in one last look of his beloved house he said in a quiet and faint voice just what he had heard the bird say to him "Open the window."

Death stopped cold where stood. He looked down at our friend, the man, and grew very furious as he screamed "WHAT! What are you saying?"

When the old man spoke, it came out more like a question. "Open the window?"

He said it so faint that neither you nor I would have heard it, but he spoke the words for Death and he heard it loud and clear.

Death whirled around in anger and stomping through the house crashed through the front door. He stormed down the garden trail and out the garden gate, letting it slam shut behind him. He went on down the road angrier than he had ever been.

As soon as Death was gone, our friend started feeling better. That ominous and oppressive feeling had left when Death departed. He sat up in the bed and he had a few handfuls of birdseed in his pocket. He put them out on the windowsill and the birds were chirping and singing for him even louder.

The man stopped and he thought. He said, "You know, I guess that is what my father said. I even think I now remember my mother telling me about it once. The day I was born my father was so happy he said 'Open the window. Let the sun shine down on my newborn boy.'"

The man lived for many years after that, celebrating each and every spring with the birds, flowers, and animals. He spent every minute he could in his garden with his friends and if anyone ever stopped by to visit he'd tell them the story of the brush he had with Death — and he was sure to tell them how his friends, the birds, saved him and how they were the family that he really needed.

Hummingbird Cake

Ingredients:

Unsalted butter, for greasing

2-3/4 cups all-purpose flour, plus more for dusting

1 cup of pecan pieces

3 ripe bananas, chopped

1/2 cup of finely chopped fresh pineapple

1/2 teaspoon of freshly grated nutmeg

1/2 teaspoon of freshly grated ginger

1/2 teaspoon of freshly grated cinnamon

1/2 teaspoon of salt

1-1/4 teaspoons of baking soda

3 large eggs, at room temperature

1-3/4 cups of granulated sugar

1 cup of vegetable oil

Directions:

Preheat the oven to 350 degrees Fahrenheit

Butter two 8-inch round cake pans and line with parchment paper

Butter the parchment and dust with flour

Spread the pecans on a baking sheet and bake until fragrant and toasted, about 8 minutes

Let cool and then roughly chop

Toss with the bananas, pineapple, and 1/2 cup flour in a small bowl

Whisk the remaining 2 1/4 cups flour, the cinnamon, nutmeg, ginger, baking soda and salt in a bowl

Beat the eggs and granulated sugar in a separate bowl with a mixer on high speed until thick and light, 5 minutes

Gradually beat in the vegetable oil

Sprinkle the flour mixture over the egg mixture, and then gently fold to make a thick batter

Fold in the pecan-fruit mixture, and then transfer the batter to the prepared pans

Bake until the cakes are firm and a toothpick inserted into the middle comes out clean, about 50 to 55 minutes

Cool in the pans on a rack for at least 25 minutes, and then invert the cakes onto the rack to cool completely

Frosting

Ingredients:

    2 packages of cream cheese (8 ounces each), at room temperature

    12 tablespoons of unsalted butter, cubed, at room temperature

    2 cups of confectioners' sugar

    1 tablespoon of finely grated lemon zest

    1 teaspoon of vanilla extract

Directions:

    Beat the cream cheese in a large bowl with a mixer until fluffy, and then gradually beat in the butter until combined

    Sift the confectioners' sugar over the cream cheese mixture and beat until smooth

    Add the lemon zest and vanilla and beat until light and fluffy

    Place one cake layer on a serving plate

    Spread about half of the frosting on top, and then cover with the other cake layer

    Spread the remaining frosting over the top and sides of the cake

Notes from Cyn:

I love this story because I spend many happy hours in my flower garden enjoying the birds. I have heard variations of this old Richard Kennedy story told by many storytellers for decades. This is my adaptation...I hope you enjoy it!

My family went to a small Lutheran Church near our house. There were many family gatherings and activities held there. The ladies and men of the church were such wonderful cooks. You can imagine the bountiful feasts we would frequently share. My mother seemed to always be baking something good to take to church. My brothers and I would whine when she'd take yet another one of her beautiful cakes out the door, leaving us with not even a morsel.

At holiday time, my mother had to lock all the newly baked Christmas cookies in the trunk of her car so we wouldn't eat them too soon, because we had found her hiding places in years past! A few years ago my younger brother had us all laughing at a family gathering. He confessed that he would sometimes carefully cut off the bottom of one of Mom's finished round layer cakes, eat the big piece, and then fix the icing so no one knew the difference, especially Momma. We laughed and laughed as Momma said that she always wondered why her cakes didn't rise like they should!

The caring and friendships made during those many years at church have sustained my mother. She is handicapped now and can't bake or go to church as she once did. However, she is still close friends with the ladies. They gather for meals and activities and take care of each other like family.

4 | GINGERBREAD MAN

A Well-loved Tale with a Recipe for Molasses Sugar Cookies

Now this one is an old, old, old folktale told for centuries by families to their children. It is especially told around the holidays, but honestly between you and me, anytime is a good time for gingerbread.

The husband was busy outside with his winter chores so the wife decided that now was as good a time as any to make gingerbread cookies. She liked to make them every year and she would always make enough to share with everyone she knew. The wife was well aware that all her family and friends thought that her gingerbread cookies were the best, so she made her dough, mixed the spices in, kneaded it all together, and got it ready by rolling it out. Now she was all set for the best part — making the nice plump, delicious cookies. She cut out giant gingerbread boys and girls because those were her favorite shapes, they were her husband's favorite shape; in fact, they were the favorite shapes of all of their friends and family. Not plain old gingerbread, but gingerbread cookies.

The wife laid them out on her old, old cookie sheet. She opened up her old oven, ready to slide the sheet on in, when suddenly to her surprise up jumped one of the gingerbread boys right off the baking sheet.

He shot off halfway across the room, turned, and looked the wife right in the eye. He said, "Nan, na, ne nan. Run, run as fast as you can, you can't catch me, I'm the gingerbread man." With that, off he went a-running right out the door.

The wife was so startled that she hollered for her husband. You could see the pair of them hobbling after the gingerbread man on down the road because they were a bit old with the rheumatism and the arthritis. That gingerbread cookie was indeed running down the dirt road as fast as he could go.

Well, it was so astonishing a sight to see that when they ran by the cows in the pasture, the cows started chasing the couple and the gingerbread boy as well — and the whole time the gingerbread cookie was singing "Nan, na, ne nan. Run, run as fast as you can, you can't catch me, I'm the gingerbread man."

As the group ran, they ran past a whole herd of horses that had been grazing. The horses took up chase too. Now it was the cows, the horses, and the husband and wife chasing the gingerbread cookie who was singing the whole time "Nan, na, ne nan. Run, run as fast as you can, you can't catch me, I'm the gingerbread man."

The odd mob ran past the whole village as they ran through town. They were trailing behind them with the cows and the horses and now everyone from town was following after that rogue gingerbread cookie.

Up ahead, they could see the river. The wife said, "Ah ha, this is it. He won't be smart enough to know you can't go swimming if you're a gingerbread boy cookie." To her surprise, though, when he got there, he gave a giant leap—BOING!—and landed on the head of a fox who just happened to be sitting there beside the river.

As he stood there atop the fox's head, the cookie said, "Take me across the river and I'll give you a good taste of gingerbread." The gingerbread man was thinking that he would just give the fox a little taste of his toe leaving him still very handsome indeed. The fox agreed to this offer and waded on into the water with the gingerbread man standing on top of him. He slowly started swimming across the river.

Seeing this happen stopped the whole crowd in their tracks — the husband and the wife, the horses and the cows, and the entire village. They all stood there staring as the gingerbread boy got away from them riding on the head of the fox. They could still hear him singing his taunting song "Nan, na, ne nan. Run, run as fast as you can, you can't catch me, I'm the gingerbread man."

As the fox was just about to reach the other bank of the river, before the whole crowd's wondering eyes, they saw him turn his crafty head and smile. He was up to something. "I'll take my taste of gingerbread now." He opened his mouth wide and CHOMP! ate the gingerbread man in one bite. Yum, yum, yum. The fox smacked at his lips the rest of the way as he swam to the bank and walked up to the other side. The whole crowd cheered and applauded. They felt that the gingerbread man had gotten what he deserved, and I'll tell you this when they all got back to the house they all wanted one of the gingerbread cookies that the wife was well known for baking. The wife was more than happy to give them all one, though they each were sure to say to her, "Please, don't make it so big and please don't make it quite so smart. In fact don't make it smart at all. We just want to eat a sweet little cookie."

And that's just what she did from then on out.

The gingerbread man was certainly a sight to behold as he ran away.

Molasses Sugar Cookies

Ingredients:

3/4 cup of shortening
2 teaspoons of baking soda
1 cup of sugar
1/2 teaspoon of cloves
1/2 teaspoon of ginger
1 teaspoon of vanilla
1 teaspoon of cinnamon
1 egg
1/2 teaspoon of salt
1/4 cup molasses
a little extra sugar
2 cups of flour

Directions:

Melt shortening and let it cool
Mix the shortening together with the sugar, egg, vanilla, and molasses
Add in dry ingredients
Refrigerate the mix for 2 hours
Form into little balls and then roll them in sugar
Bake on a greased cookie sheet for 8-10 minutes at 350 degrees
These will disappear so fast you may want to do a double batch!

Notes from Cyn:

Before modern day stores and markets, families here in the South had to make their own molasses. We once went to a fall harvest party up in the country of Stokes County. Bruce's friend grew sugar cane and in the fall when the crop "came in" it was time to cook. Folks came from miles around to help with the harvest and molasses making. The sugar cane was boiled with water in huge flat pans over a fire or special burner. The cooking and stirring went on for hours which left lots of time for stories, home cooking, moonshine drinking, and tall tale telling. When the mixture was thick and dark the molasses was ready to be put in jars to use all year long. We brought home mason jars of that thick, sweet, dark syrup to eat for the whole winter.

The gingerbread made by the bakers at Old Salem in North Carolina is a centuries' old recipe and a local favorite. The Old Guilford Mill has a terrific mix for sale to bake your own old-time gingerbread with the flour ground right there at the mill. The site dates back to the Revolutionary War.

5 | STONE SOUP

A Tale of Community Spirit with a Recipe for a New England Boiled Dinner

This story is an old favorite of mine. In modern times, it has a wonderful message for everyone to share.

It had been a hard, hard winter. The fall harvest had not been a fruitful one, so when folks began trying to eat what they had raised, even getting down to the root cellar, there was not much left by the dead of winter.

An emergency town meeting was called. "What will we do?" The villagers got together talking on the matter and soon everyone was worrying about it because no one had any answers. The war had come and gone and it had been hard on the families, so no one had very much money or very much food. Many families were still grieving losses. It was a sad, sad time.

One day a little boy was walking around and he found the prettiest stone he had ever seen. It was round and looked like marble, but it wasn't. It looked like a gem, but it wasn't. He thought to himself, "Ya know, this looks like a magic stone. I think I am going to take it home to my grandmamma." That's just what he did.

Grandmamma smiled when he put it into her withered old hand. She said to her grandson, "My dear I think you have found a magic stone indeed. Let's make some soup with it for supper because everyone is hungry."

The boy didn't question her. Why would he? After all, she was his grandmamma and she was old and wise and loved him very much. They went outside and built a fire underneath the big, old pot. They filled it with water from the creek and got it boiling. Then the boy threw in his magic stone and let it simmer and simmer. Grandmamma had a few herbs left in her pots, so she threw in a wee bit of rosemary and a wee bit of thyme and of course she had to put in some of her basil. It simmered some more. By then it smelled so delicious that they decided to have a wee bit of a party for themselves. They figured it would taste great and be the best stone soup that anyone had ever made.

A neighbor was coming along down the road and said, "Oh my, are we having a gathering? I would love to help with the soup. I have just one small shriveled potato." She went and got it and put it in the stew, and they stirred and stirred and stirred until it was even more fragrant and delicious smelling.

About that time, a farmer from down the road came walking by and said, "Oh, oh, that soup of yours is smelling very flavorsome." Grandmamma explained that they were making magic stone soup. The farmer said, "I know what would be very tasty in it. I have just a small piece of bacon left from last harvest." He brought it over and indeed it was very small, but he placed it in the soup all the same. Oh, the aroma! How good it all smelled! It was drawing folks in from everywhere, and the people coming home from the market all added a little bit of this and a little bit of that, each one put in some turnips, some shriveled carrots, some celery, some onions, some beans, some mushrooms, and even a little bit of meat. One woman had some delicious smelling and aromatic marjoram herb. She put it in and that made all the difference.

Soon a crowd had gathered in front of the house and everyone was complementing the boy for finding the magic stone, and his grandmamma was smiling because by now the huge pot was bubbling and delicious smelling. When she ladled the soup into bowls, they had to borrow bowls from this family and that family because so many people had contributed to the soup. Each ladle of soup was filled with delicious vegetables and a wee bit of this and a wee bit of that.

They had enough of that delicious fragrant soup for the whole community that had gathered. They ate and smiled and talked with one another. Soon there was singing and instruments came out to be played, so naturally dancing followed. The storytelling was just as lively and continued into the night. It was the happiest any of them had been in a long, long time.

That night when they went to bed, Grandmamma was tucking her little grandson in and she said to him, "You know, you are such a wise boy. I'm so glad you brought home that magic stone. You're smarter than many, many older people."

The boy smiled and said, "Yes, and so are you Grandmamma, cause you believe in magic."

From that time on, each spring the community would have a Magic Stone Soup gathering. The party lasted sometimes for days and even when prosperity came back to the village and the men returned home from war and everyone was in much better spirits they continued to have the big pot of Magic Stone Soup and, when doing so, they also made sure that everyone, even the youngest, was allowed to put something in the soup.

The magic stone helped to feed a community in need and
renew their spirits.

New England Boiled Dinner

Ingredients:

- 1 large beef roast
- 3 or more large onions, quartered
- 1 eight ounce bag of small carrots (already cleaned)
- 3 or 4 medium new potatoes, cut in half
- 2 cloves of garlic
- 1 teaspoon of thyme
- 1 bay leaf
- 2 sprigs of rosemary
- Pepper and salt to taste
- 1-2 quarts of chicken broth or stock (enough to cover the meat well)

Directions:

Cook the beef for about 1 hour with the stock
Bring to a boil then reduce heat to a simmer
Add all the vegetables and more stock
Add the cabbage and the herbs last
Cover and simmer until the vegetables are soft

Notes from Cyn:

This was one of my Daddy's favorite meals so we had it often. My Mom called it New England Boiled Dinner but she learned it from her family in Ohio and she cooked it in North Carolina, so what does that tell ya? Whatever the name, it was a good hearty meal! It sounds like an age old recipe that would have been cooked over the open fireplace in Colonial America times. We like to do it in the crock pot beginning on high heat for the first two hours with two to three cans of beer instead of chicken stock. Then I add everything else and enough chicken stock to cover the vegetables then cook on medium for two hours. If you add too much liquid it might over flow! This is a great one pot meal. I dice the leftovers, add a large can of cooked, diced tomatoes, and simmer for half an hour to make vegetable soup.

6 | THE MAGIC POT

A Traditional Tale with a Recipe for Oxtail Stew

Once upon a time there was a husband and a wife who lived deep in the forest in a tiny little house. They loved each other very, very much. They always had whatever they wanted that was good to eat and made with lots and lots of love.

One day it was getting close to her birthday and the husband wanted to get his wife a special present. He thought to himself, "I think I'll make her one. She loves all of her cooking, so I think I'll get her something for the kitchen."

Now, you have to remember, that long ago, did they have fancy stoves and microwaves? No, they didn't, so the husband had to go searching in the forest for something. He looked and looked, and he looked some more, but he didn't see anything. Just as he was about to give up, he decided to try just one more time and that was the trick because that's when he saw it — just over there, buried in the leaves, it was the rim of a cook pot. It was one of those big, black, heavy kinds; the type that you would make soup or stew in or something yummy for dinner. He decided that was what he needed and he dug it up and pulled it out of the ground.

When he got it out, he looked it over and decided it was perfect because she did not have a pot this big to cook in the fireplace. Yes, he decided, this present was going to be absolutely divine. He cleaned it up singing, "Scrub banana, rub banana / Scrub banana, rub banana / Scrub banana, rub banana," until it was nice and shiny. He wrapped it up in wrapping paper and then ran all the way home.

When he got home, he was so excited that he could not wait for her birthday to surprise her. He said, "Honey, I have something for you." When she came around, he gave her a big hug and a big kiss and said "I got your birthday present for you early, something I kind of fixed up."

The wife accepted the present and took the wrapping off and when she saw the shiny black pot she simply loved it. "Oh, my gracious! It's just what I wanted!" She started crying happy tears and hugging her husband and kissed him again and again.

When she was finally finished thanking her husband, she pulled up the heavy big, black pot and put it by the fire. "My goodness, what should I make for supper? I do believe that I have wanted to make some of that delicious potato soup that my papa gave me the recipe for so many years ago, and it's just perfect for this pot."

So she got herself a potato and washed it off and peeled it and then got the fire going in the fireplace. She put the pot close enough to the fire so the water in it would get nice and hot and pretty soon would begin to boil. The wife decided that rather than chop up the potato like her papa's recipe said to do, that she would leave it whole and put it in the pot—kerplunk. Then she went and got herself another potato, washed it off real good, peeled it and went to go drop it in the pot—but wait a minute. There in the pot was not just one potato but two! "How did this happen?" she exclaimed. "I know I just put one potato in there, and here is the second one in my hand. But all together now I have three potatoes. Well my goodness gracious, this is very strange." Unsure of what was going on, she called out to her husband for help.

The husband heard his wife calling for help and came as quick as he could. "Whatever is the matter my darling?"

"Well, you're not going to believe it," exclaimed the wife, her voice full of raw excitement, "but this pot is incredible. It made a potato."

The husband looked at his wife for a moment before finally repeating the words that she said. "The pot made a potato?"

"I know it's very strange indeed," said the wife, "but who knew there was such a thing as a pot that made potatoes." With that, she dropped the second one in the pot right then and there in front of her husband to see what would happen—kerplunk—and dipped in her big cooking spoon and when she pulled it out she had four potatoes.

The wife let loose with such a gleeful cry of joy. Never before was such a sound heard. "Ah, this wonderful pot!" she exclaimed. "It's so special; I know exactly what we can do with it! We could invite all our relatives over for supper!"

The husband, though, was a much more sober thinker than his wife. "Now wait just a moment there my dear," he said to her. "Maybe it can make two of anything. Let's put one of something else in there and see what happens."

The wife nodded her head in agreement and began thinking what else they could put in there, but the husband already had an idea. A long time ago, back when he was a boy, his grandfather had given him a tiny little piece of gold. He went to his room, fished it out of its hiding place, and came running to his wife and the big, black pot. He showed it to her and then before she could speak, dropped it in—kerplunk.

Together they waited a few anxious moments, and then, using the wife's big cooking spoon, dipped it in and pulled out not one piece of gold but two!

The couple was so excited they could hardly stand it! They began to jump up and down in joy. Then they had an idea. They put the two pieces of gold in the magic pot—kerplunk. A moment later, they used the big cooking spoon and pulled out four pieces of gold. They put the four pieces of gold in the pot—kerplunk. They used the spoon and pulled out eight pieces of gold. They put the eight pieces of gold in the pot—kerplunk and using the spoon they pulled out sixteen pieces of gold.

They kept it up all night. They would put the gold in and use the big cooking spoon to pull out twice as much. They did it until they had gold piled up everywhere in their tiny little house. They had gold in the kitchen, gold in the parlor. They had gold in the bedroom and in the bathroom, why they even had gold on the back porch.

"This is all so exciting!" cried the wife to her husband. "Let's go shopping!"

The husband and wife went down to the village and immediately began buying all the things they had ever wanted—just buying, buying, buying, buying, buying, and more buying. When they got home, the husband spent that evening making even more gold. The next day they went back into town and brought more...and more, and more, and more, and more, and more. Pretty soon they had to buy a great big house just to hold all the things they had purchased. They had horses and carriages and the neighbors were saying amongst themselves, "What is happening here?"

It didn't take too long until everyone in town was talking about it. The wife was going to church in long, beautiful, flowing gowns and was making everyone jealous. She was wearing so much jewelry too; rings, bracelets, and necklaces — after all, the pot made twice the number of anything.

Then one night, as the couple sat down for supper, the husband sadly said to his wife "We haven't had a walk in the woods in a long time. You haven't given me a hug after supper in a long time."

The wife wasn't really listening to what her husband was saying, though. "Oh, but we're having such wonderful suppers, why, just look at this magnificent meal that the cook has made for us."

The husband sadly shook his head and said, "I miss some of the things back from when we were living in that tiny little house."

The wife snapped at him and said, "Oh, don't be silly. Go down to the basement and make more gold."

After eating their tasty supper, later that night the husband went downstairs to the basement where they kept the magic pot and made more gold like his wife asked him to do. He put it in and pulled it out, over and over again until all of a sudden—Splash—the husband fell in the pot. His legs were kicking up in the air and he screamed the whole time he tried to get out.

The wife heard all the noise and she came running down the stairs saying, "Oh, my darling, wait a moment, let me help you." She raced over to the magic pot, took hold of her husband, and using all her strength, managed to pull him out. As they stood there next to each other, they leaned over and looked into the pot and saw two more legs sticking out! The wife leaned over, grabbed the legs, and began to pull as hard as she could until a second husband popped out.

Goodness gracious! Now the wife had two husbands, identical twins — same hair, same eyes, same clothes, and the same sad frown.

Who knew that this simple find could lead to such mayhem? The poor husband certainly didn't!

The wife became hysterical and started to panic, crying out, "What are we going to do? We can't just have husbands popping up everywhere. What will people say? Oh, this is just terrible!" She was in such a state that she was jumping up and down and all of a sudden—Splash—she fell in the pot.

Of course, the husbands rushed over and pulled her out. When they were finished, they pulled the second wife out too, and she had the same hair, same clothes, and same tears.

"Oh this is just awful!" exclaimed one of the wives. "Don't anyone get near that pot. What are we going to do?"

Well, all night long the two couples worried and talked and tried to figure out what to do. The wives were worried about what people would say and the husbands reminded them about how much happier they were before the magic pot was found. That was when they finally had a good idea.

The two couples went back upstairs to their great big beautiful kitchen where there was an old book filled with wisdom. They knew that books were good places to go to for looking up the answers to problems that people can have and sure enough, that was where they found their answer.

The next day the two sets of couples got all dressed up and looked very nice as they set out to go down to the village and have a bite to eat with their friends before heading off to church. They didn't say a word to anybody. They didn't tell anybody who the extra set of husband and wife were; they just went right on into the church and sat down.

After church everybody had thought, without even thinking too hard about it, that the extra she must have been the wife's long-lost twin sister. "Oh, how nice to meet you my dear," the ladies of the church said as they went up and introduced themselves to her. "And you," they said as they addressed the extra he, "must be the husband's long-lost twin brother. So happy to meet you too. Welcome to the community!" It was amazing, but nobody ever knew the difference.

The husband and wife built their identical twins a great big house just like theirs and they would get together every night for supper, but, just to be extra careful, one night, they took the pot, all four of them, into the woods. There, they dug a deep, deep hole. They put the pot in the hole and covered it up so no one would ever find it again. They had enough trouble out of that pot and they had learned that love and friendship was a lot more important than all the money in the world. They had learned the lesson that sometimes one is enough and two is sometimes one too many.

Oxtail Stew

Ingredients:

8 slices of cooked bacon, chopped, be sure to save the drippings

Olive oil

3 large sprigs of rosemary

2 large bay leaves

1 tablespoon plus 1-1/2 cups of all-purpose flour

1 tablespoon of butter

2 tablespoons of salt

1/2 tablespoon of black pepper

4 to 4-1/2 pounds of oxtail pieces, trimmed of excess fat

2 cups of chopped onion

1 cup of diced carrot plus 6 medium carrots cut into large chunks

4 large garlic cloves

2-3/4 cups of beef broth

1 pound of baby Bella mushrooms, cut into quarters

4 onions cut into eights

Directions:

Cook the bacon in a heavy pot until crispy, transfer to a plate and pour the drippings into a small bowl, mix with olive oil so that you have 6 tablespoons

Tie together the herbs into a bouquet

Stir 1 tablespoon of flour and butter into a smooth paste then set aside

Combine 1-1/2 cups of flour, 2 tablespoons of salt, 1/2 tablespoon of black pepper into a medium bowl; add the oxtails and toss to evenly coat. Discard the remaining flour mixture.

Heat the bacon drippings over a medium heat and brown the ox tails on all sides

Remove the oxtails and set aside

Reduce heat and add the chopped onions, diced carrots, and minced garlic for about five minutes.

Return the oxtails back to the pot adding the herb bouquet and the broth

Cover and gently simmer for about 2 hours

Mix in the mushrooms, carrot chunks and more onions and garlic if desired

Return to a boil; reduce heat to low and let simmer for about another hour

Spoon off any fat on the surface

Directions continued on following page

Stir flour paste into the stew
Simmer for another half hour with the cover off until the stew thickens
Break up the pieces of meat before serving.
Some cooks like to serve this dish over noodles or mashed potatoes.
If you like you can substitute ham for oxtails

Notes from Cyn:

I have a German friend, Solly, who loves to cook. She gave me the oxtail recipe, which reminded me so much of our old family favorite. When my brothers and I were little in the 1950s, my mother made this recipe with a ham bone instead of oxtails. We frequently had navy bean soup cooked with a ham bone. A big pot of this filling, savory soup was a cheap way to feed a hungry family of four and the leftovers lasted for days. She'd serve it with diced onion on top. My daddy loved catsup, so he'd put catsup in the soup too. When we were tired of the soup, Momma made the best traditional tomato based baked beans from the last of the bean soup. Mom was a "stay-at-home wife" who prided herself on a spotless home and good home cooking. There wasn't much choice because there weren't any "fast food" eating places. It is amazing to me that my mother and the other military wives in our Camp Lejeune Base trailer park created these memorable family meals in tiny kitchens with no electric kitchen aids. There were no dishwashers, electric can openers, toaster ovens, or microwaves. Yet around that small dinette table we laughed, talked, and told stories.

7 | THE FAT CAT

A Danish Tale with a Recipe for Danish Fontina Cheese, Ham, and Eggs Omelet

It was after school and back in those days children played together a lot. They went outside, they had fun with their friends, and they would play make-believe. Of course they always did their homework first, but on this one particular day, while they were inside finishing up their homework, Mom said, "I'm going next-door to the neighbors.' I'll be right back. Make sure you give Kitty some milk and finish your homework before you all go outside to play."

Of course, being such well-behaved children, they said "yes." As they finished their homework, Kitty was beginning to look a wee bit hungry and started meowing. She wanted some milk, so they gave her milk. After that, she was meowing even more than before. She wanted even more milk and now she wanted food as well, so they gave her some more milk. They didn't notice at first, but, surprisingly enough, Kitty looked like she was getting a wee bit bigger.

When they weren't looking, Kitty turned around and ate a whole loaf of bread that was sitting on top of the counter cooling for supper, and while they were working on their books Kitty went and ate a pie that mamma had baked for the church supper. Kitty was indeed now looking bigger, noticeably. As the children looked at kitty, they noticed that she was getting so big that she was beginning to get a sinister look to her. She was no longer looking like their sweet Kitty that they loved. Kitty turned around and before the children's astonished eyes she opened up the cupboard and she started eating everything she could get her paws on, boxes and all.

"Stop, Kitty, stop! Mamma is going to be so upset. She is going to be blaming us. Stop, Kitty, stop!" the children cried out in fear and panic at her.

Kitty, though, kept eating and eating and eating. Soon she was as tall as they were. By now the children were in quite a panic. They were about to race out the door when all of a sudden Kitty got extra hungry and—gulp!—she ate the little boy. And —gulp!—she ate the little girl. Kitty was still hungry — even after eating all the food in the house, including the little boy and the little girl — and so she tromped out the door and went next-door.

By now she was *soooo* big Kitty could barely fit through the door. She went to the neighbor's and she ate all of their food — and then she ate the family. By now Kitty was really huge; she was a giant of a cat and was still hungry.

Everyone in the village was running from Kitty, they were afraid that they were going to be next. As they ran from her, they shouted, "Kitty, Kitty, go away!", but she came running at them because she was still hungry.

Just as she was about to open up her giant jaws and eat another house and the people in it, a little dog from down the road woke up from his little nap from underneath a little tree. He saw what was happening and he knew exactly what he had to do. In his big, big voice, he started barking as loud as he could and he barked at Kitty—woof-woof-woof-woof. He barked as loud as a big dog could. He barked so loud that he sounded like a great, big dog.

Kitty spun on her heals and took a quick look around. Not even seeing the dog, she became so frightened that she started running in the opposite direction as fast as she could go. She was running and running and running. Being scared as she was, she was not looking where she was going. Kitty tripped—boing!—and fell flat.

And when she did her big mouth opened up and out flew the little boy—whoosh—and out flew the little girl—whoosh—out flew the pie, out flew the cake, out flew the next-door neighbors, out flew the house—whoosh, whoosh, whoosh, whoosh—until everyone was back where they should be and Kitty had shrunk back down to normal size.

The dog was chasing her around the house barking his head off, but Mamma didn't stop him like she usually would have. Instead she got everyone settled back down and sat them down for supper. Mamma said to her family, "From now on we are not going to feed Kitty anything but a little milk and a little cat food and keep her on a strict, strict diet."

This hungry, giant of a cat, who used to be a family's
loving pet, terrorized a community for a time.

Danish Fontina Cheese, Ham, and Eggs Omelet

Ingredients:

2 cups of Danish Fontina cheese

1 pound of ham minced

12 large eggs

1 tablespoon of butter

1/2 teaspoon of salt and pepper

Directions:

Pre-heat oven to 400 degrees Fahrenheit

Melt oil and butter in a 12 inch skillet with an ovenproof handle

Cook diced ham slowly for about 3 minutes or until browned

Whisk eggs, salt, pepper, and milk together

Pour egg mixture over the ham in the skillet and cook until the eggs are setting up and getting a little brown on the bottom

Remove from heat and put whole skillet in the oven for about 10 minutes

Remove from oven and sprinkle the cheese evenly over the entire pan

Return to the oven for 3 or so minutes to melt the cheese

Notes from Cyn:

This is so hearty even the Fat Cat would have enough to eat! I sometimes add mushrooms, garlic, chopped onions, or leeks to sauté before the ham. The popular sweet Danish specialties include cheese. These are, of course, the "cheese Danish" or "Danish coffee cake." Ham and cheese are also frequently found in Danish recipes.

This folktale has a theme that can be found in many cultures. An animal or person eats an improbable amount, grows to exaggerated size, and then the victims are saved in some way. Sody Sallyratus is an American example. I like the happy endings of these two. Some can be classified as Tall Tales depending on how exaggerated the eating. Some cultures use these as simple cautionary stories about the perils of gluttony and over-eating.

8 | THREE WISHES

A German Tale with a Recipe for Hot German Saluda Cole Slaw

Once upon a time long ago and far away, there lived a husband and a wife. They had been together for so many years and now they were comfortable with each other. They had kind of gotten past the romantic "I love you" time of life. Unfortunately, they were not doing well financially. The husband had not been working, the fields were barren, and they didn't have much food at all. One night, when they sat down to supper, all there was to split between them was a potato and a mere, tiny little sausage.

The husband said, "Is this all there is for dinner? Can't you find something else?"

"No," said the wife sadly, "that's all there is."

Well, the husband was so frustrated that he went to bed hungry. He thought about their situation all night; he tossed and turned and dreamed about sausages. HA! What a thing to dream about.

The next day the husband went down to the village to try to sell some of his straw. He packed it up high on his old mule. As he traveled, he happened upon a bent, old, crippled looking woman sitting beside the side of the road. Now, he knew everybody in these parts, but she... well, she was different. He had never seen her before and didn't know who she was.

Everyone is friendly in the South, and they were back then too so he said to her, "Hello, how are you?"

The woman could barely speak, but managed to say in a pitiful tone, "I am very tired. Do you have anything you can spare? A sip of water? Anything?"

The husband didn't hesitate and said, "Well, yes. I don't have any food, but I would be glad to share my water with you." With that he got out his canteen of water and shared it with her.

As the man turned to leave, the old woman said to him, "You are a good soul. You're a good man. Here's what I would like to give to you. I would like to give to you this," and she handed the husband a strange little looking round pot. It had a lid that opened, but when he looked in, there was nothing inside.

The husband was a polite man and smiled at her, thanking her for the gift; he then went on to the market to try to sell his bundles of straw. While he was there, he even had the idea of trying to sell the little pot the woman had given him, but nobody at the market wanted to buy it, not at any price.

On his way back home, the husband was sad because he had made no money. He had not managed to sell anything, not his straw nor the little pot. As he traveled, he saw the same bent, old, crippled looking woman still sitting beside the side of the road. This time she looked a little bit better than she had earlier in the day. She said to the husband as he passed by "Your goodness to me has made me feel so much better. I was just looking for a stranger to help me. Because of this, I'm going to tell you that the pot I gave you contains three wishes."

"Oh," the husband exclaimed, "three wishes! That would be wonderful."

"Go now my friend," said the old woman. "Go in peace."

The husband hurried on home, he could hardly wait to tell his wife. When he arrived home, he burst into the house and exclaimed, "Look, dear, look what I've got! I have a magical pot that contains three wishes!" He was so happy and excited. "Now what are we going to wish for first?"

Well, the husband and wife argued back and forth all night over what to wish for. The wife wanted a great big mansion and a great big pile of gold, but as they went on and on, the husband grew hungrier and hungrier. Finally, without thinking, he just sighed out in a moan of hunger and frustration, "I just wish I had a plate of sausages. I am so tired of not having sausages; I wish that you had a sausage on the end of your nose."

SNAP! Just like that, there appeared on the table before him a big plate of delicious sausages, but also just as quickly SNAP! There was a sausage hanging off of the poor wife's nose.

"ARG!" cried the wife. "This is terrible, what am I going to do? What will I tell my friends? I look awful!" She cried and cried.

The husband didn't know what to say to his wife so he tried the best he could. "Oh, it's not that bad, you look fine." He decided to try to make it up to her and wished for what she wanted, a huge mansion filled with gold — and just like that SNAP! They had the mansion and it was filled with gold. The husband thought that from there on out everything would be alright. He even hired servants for his wife so that she could better enjoy their new life together, but the wife was miserable and sad. "This sausage," she cried "I can't go to church looking like this. I can't have parties. I can't even have friends come over. I look terrible!"

The husband tried talking to her about trying to make the best of it. He put a veil over her head. He tried to hide the sausage behind a scarf. He did all these things for her. They even went places with her looking like that, but when they did everyone saw the sausage and laughed and laughed and laughed. No one wished for their terrible luck, to have all that money and nice big house, but to still be so miserable and sad all the time.

This pot – and a man's hunger – caused grief to his poor wife.

Day after day the wife wandered through the lush and lavish rooms of her gold encrusted mansion, unable to enjoy anything. Nothing brought her any joy. She was the saddest creature her husband had ever seen.

With a long and heavy sigh, the husband said, "You know wife, I just do not know what I am going to do. I would gladly give it all back, the house and the gold, if only you could be happy again."

The husband truly did love his dear wife, and he truly did not want her to be so sad and miserable. He truly did mean the words that he spoke, and just like that SNAP! The sausage was off of her nose — and there together they stood, back in their little old house in their old and worn-out clothes. Next to them on the table, was the plate with the sausage on it. That night, they sat down at the table and shared it together, and were more than happy to do so. For you see, the husband and the wife finally realized that it was more important that they had the love of each other than the nicest house filled with gold.

Hot German Saluda Cole Slaw

This recipe goes great with German sausages

Ingredients:

1 large head of cabbage, finely shredded
3 large onions, sliced thin
1 cup of oil
1 cup of vinegar
1 cup of sugar
1 tablespoon of mustard
1 tablespoon of celery seed
1 tablespoon of salt

Directions:

Mix onions and cabbage then sprinkle with salt
Bring other ingredients to a boil and then remove from heat and let it cool
Mix it all together
Put it in a dish with a cover and place it in the refrigerator for twenty-four hours before serving
This dish will keep in the refrigerator for four or five days. It can also be frozen

Notes from Cyn:

Germany is our most frequent European travel destination. The Bavarian countryside, warm people, and fascinating history are favorites of Fred's and mine, but it is the cuisine that we love the most. Rustic, hearty fare brings their families together. It was not until I first went to Germany that I learned that there were so many different kinds of sausages. They had whole cases filled with them: Bratwurst, Braunschweiger, Bregenwurst, Gelbwurst, Kalbsleberwurst, Knackwurst, Landjäger, Leberkäse, Leberwurst, Nürnberger Rostbratwurst, Rostbratwurst, Teewurst, Thüringer Rostbratwurst, and Weiwurst, which is also known as "white sausage." This story just tickles my fancy; maybe because it reminds me of my own silly husband, Fred. I think that he would do something like the husband in this story because he likes sausages and German food with excellent beer so much.

9 | LAZY, LAZY

An Old Folk Tale with a Recipe for the Moore Family Potato Soup

Long ago and far away there once lived a couple at the edge of their farm. The husband was very good looking and very charming. Unfortunately he was also a wee bit lazy. He tried, but he was very tired most of the time. This was alright, though, since his wife, who loved him, worked hard enough for both of them.

One day while out in the garden the wife was working too hard and pulled something in her back. She went hobbling into the house like an old crone even though she was a young woman. She said to her husband, "My darling, you're going to have to go out and work in the garden for us. I can't. My back is bad, I hurt it and now I must lie down to rest and heal."

Of course the husband couldn't say no, but he went out there very unenthusiastically. He hoed a little bit here and pulled some weeds there. Soon, he sat down on a stump to rest. It was then that he was thinking to himself, "Ya know, Saint Patrick's Day is coming soon and I've heard all those legends about if you ever capture a leprechaun you get a wish. I'd wish for a pot of gold. Maybe I'll start looking for a leprechaun."

This he did. Each day he would go out and work in the garden just a little bit. He would look and look and one day he was finally rewarded when he heard some whistling. It got louder and louder. He peered out from behind a potato plant and indeed there he was — a real live leprechaun. He had a tall green hat, a green jacket, a green shirt, green britches, green socks, green boots, and even green underwear.

He stood there and watched for a moment; then he slowly crept up behind the leprechaun and quick as can be he reached out and grabbed him. The leprechaun jumped, but was too slow and was caught. Pleading, he said, "Let me go, let me go, HELP!"

The husband farmer said, "I'm not going to hurt you; I'll just let you go if you give me my wish." The man wasn't thinking of being greedy and asking for gold. The leprechaun firmly agreed by nodding his head. The husband let him go.

"Oh, that was a terrible ordeal!" said the leprechaun. "Look at me, you wrinkled my jacket. I don't know what I'm going to do. Alright now, how about the wish? I've got to be getting going, Saint Patrick's Day is coming and I'm very busy celebrating this time of year now don't ya know."

"Well, I want my wish," said the husband. "Now, let me see..."

Now you or I would wish for something like 'world peace' or 'a good crop' or 'health for everyone,' but our friend the husband was hungry. He was so hungry his stomach was rumbling — and he was so tired of working in that garden too — so without thinking he said, "I'd like a giant potato so I won't have to harvest and dig in this garden of mine for a long, long time."

The leprechaun looked at him quizzically, "A giant potato? That's your wish?"

"Yes," he said, "that's what I want. It'll please my wife, too."

"All right," said the leprechaun, "if you're sure, but you should be careful what you wish for..." With that, he—poof!—disappeared.

Well, before our friend could turn around he heard his wife and neighbors coming out of their houses. Everyone was running and screaming in shock and surprise because right there in the middle of the road was the biggest, the most giant, and the most monstrous potato you ever did see. It was taller than a house and wider than a mountain. Everyone was screaming and hollering "ARRGG!"

"What is this?" said his wife. Her husband looked so guilty that she just knew he was the cause of it. "What have you done? We got to get this out of the way. It's blocking the road."

Sure enough just about that time a wagon pulled up. They couldn't go around it, they couldn't go over it. Everyone was thoroughly angry and disgusted with our friend.

"Oh dear," said the wife, "let's do something."

She and the other neighborhood ladies went up and chopped, chopped, chopped and tried to chop off big pieces from the potato. They did.

She went in and cooked the potato bits that she chopped off. She cooked for the next ten days the potatoes that they chopped off. She cooked potato pancakes, she cooked French fries, and she cooked potato soup, mashed potatoes, scalloped potatoes, and every kind of potatoes you can think of.

About ten days later she and the ladies went out and said, "Ya know, it doesn't look any smaller to me." They all agreed, but went back to chopping and preparing potato for dinner.

About ten days after that, it STILL didn't look any smaller.

The whole county was talking about this giant potato. Everyone was glaring at her when she went to market. As for her husband—HA! They wouldn't even speak to him.

On a bright sunny day, she stood there, that pretty wife, trying to think what they could do to get rid of the potato, to get it out of their lives. As she looked at it, to her surprise, the potato was sprouting. Yes, right there was a bud—and there was a bud, and there, and there, and there. All over the potato were sprouts. My mother called them eyes and that's what they called them back then, but it gave her a good idea.

How lazy can one person be? This big, giant, and
most monstrous potato is certainly a clue!

The wife quickly went to work and, the next morning, when folks were trying to get around going to the market and going to their house and going to see their children, they saw a sign. It said: "Giant potato sprouts for sale. Have your very own giant potato."

Oh my gracious. Everyone saw this. They saw the potato and they saw the sprouts and thought to themselves what nice things this would bring. They could put the giant potato in their backyard and they would have plenty of food for the whole winter.

Soon, the wife's basket was full of glittering coins and the potato was being chopped, chopped, and chopped by everyone. They called out to all the folks walking by. People were coming from all over the county to get their magic potato sprouts.

By the end of the day the potato was small enough so that several big strong men, including her husband, could roll the potato over and finally off of the road. Everyone was happy.

It was such a relief. I don't know when she told that husband of hers about the basket filled with coins. She may have even waited a few weeks or a few months maybe even a year to start spending it here and there for a few little luxuries. Because you see, after all of this he realized that he couldn't be lazy anymore; he had to be a very busy, helpful husband to keep a smart wife like his happy.

Moore Family Potato Soup

Ingredients

- 2 tablespoons of butter
- 2 cloves of garlic
- 1 large onion, chopped
- 1 teaspoon of black pepper
- Salt if desired, about half a teaspoon
- 3 or 4 Russet or Yukon Gold potatoes, quartered
- 4 cups of chicken broth
- 1/2 a cup of cream or milk

Directions:

Sauté garlic and onion in butter until onions are translucent

Add broth and potatoes to the pan, bring to a boil, and then simmer gently until potatoes are tender

Mash the potatoes then add the milk or cream; add pepper and salt if desired and bring back to a boil

Remove from the heat

Mash everything again, mix well

Serve with crumbled bacon, croutons, grated cheese, parsley, or all of the above!

Notes from Cyn:

My family has Irish ancestry as well as German. This robust meal was a frequent Moore family favorite that has been passed down. When asked, my mother remembered making it of course, but she said that my dad would sometimes make it for the family as well. This was another popular meal to make for a frugal family of the 1950s as it is an economical, filling meal fit for a big family. Nowadays, the new celebrity television chefs prepare this dish, but when they do, some of them use leeks instead of onions. They also recommend putting the finished soup in a blender or use an immersion mixer to make the texture smoother, but we like the rustic texture better. The French version is served cold as an appetizer rather than the main meal.

10 | THE BEEKEEPER AND THE RABBIT

J. ClemBurne

A Tale from Ireland with a Recipe for Oven Baked Southern Fried Honey Chicken and Hoe Cakes

I went down to Londontown
to see the sights and look around
and all the girls came back to me
saying "Donny, where's your trousers?"
Oh the wind blows high and the wind blows low
and follows me now wherever I go
and all the girls follow after me
saying "Donny, where's your trousers?"

(An old Irish folksong teasing the Scottish men about their kilts)

The beekeeper lived in a small cottage and was very, very happy. Behind the house he had row after row of beehives. He kept beehives, but the bees weren't just bees that gave him honey, no, to the beekeeper they were like his friends and his family. He'd go out and talk to them and the bees would come out and swarm around him without stinging him. Every now and then he would harvest the honey and take it down to the market to sell. In the fall, he'd harvest the bee's wax for making candles and sell them at market.

One day, as he was coming back from the market, he noticed on his front porch a rabbit. This was very odd because the rabbit just sat there instead of hopping off or scampering away. As he walked up the steps, the rabbit turned a sweet little face up to look at him and to his surprise the eyes of the rabbit were blue. The bluest blue he's ever seen. Now he knew that rabbits didn't have blue eyes, but they just seemed to suit her; he was already thinking of the little rabbit as a girl.

He thought that she would hop away as he got closer to her, but she didn't. In fact, as he opened the door of the cottage, the little rabbit just hopped right into his house. She hopped right up on his kitchen table and watched him with those big blue eyes the whole time he fixed supper. She sat there as if she was just enjoying his company as the beekeeper ate his supper.

When he went to bed that night, he didn't put her out like he thought he should. Instead he gave the little bunny a bath and put her in a basket by the fireplace — and she lay there, cuddled down and snuggled up, and went fast to sleep.

The next morning, the rabbit sat there on the breakfast table with the beekeeper. She was just sitting there looking at him. He couldn't help himself and soon he found that he was talking to her and asking her questions. To the beekeeper, it seemed as if the rabbit could understand what he was telling her and saying. Oh, if only she could talk back.

When the beekeeper went to market the next week, he took the little rabbit with him. People were so intrigued with her blue eyes and everyone wanted to pet her. Not once did she hop out of the basket. She didn't even try to.

As the beekeeper and his bunny were leaving the market that evening, he saw a woman, an old woman staring at him. Her eyes followed him and the rabbit as they went. Then she started following them home, hobbling along the road.

The beekeeper thought this was very strange indeed as the old woman had a sinister look about her, so he hurried on home and shut the door tight before that mean-looking, old woman could get too close to them.

Next week the same thing happened when he and the rabbit went back to the market. That woman appeared and watched them the whole time. This time the beekeeper asked one of his friends, one of the market fellows, "Who is that?" and he pointed over to the old woman.

The fellow said "Oh, her." His friend's voice grew quiet and he took a few steps closer to the beekeeper. "Well, it's rumored that she is a dark, dark person. They say that she has strange ways about her and can cast strange spells. If I were you, I would stay away from her my friend."

"Indeed," the beekeeper agreed.

The bees were especially active that year. The beekeeper got lots and lots of extra honey and bee's wax from them, but autumn was on its way, the temperatures had grown cooler, the leaves were starting to fall and he had to prepare the hives for winter, making sure that they would all stay warm. He could see that the bees were staying in the hive more and more often. For everyone knows that bees do not like winter or the cold. They stay in their hives during the cold months. Bees spend most of the winter hibernating.

All the time that the beekeeper worked on getting his hives ready for the winter months the little rabbit helped him by sharing in every task. He had gotten so used to her being around him all the time; she was such a sweet companion.

One day, though, as the beekeeper went to go about his daily chores his little rabbit companion was gone. He missed her and started to worry about her, so he went looking for her — and what do you think he saw? It was none other than that creepy old woman. She was standing right there in the middle of the road just staring at his house. The beekeeper kept looking for his little rabbit and went out and saw her in the herb garden. He went right over to her, snatched her up, and took her into the house, slamming the door and locking it tight behind him. When he looked out the window to see if the coast was clear, though, that old woman was still there as creepy as ever.

Winter was coming, it was almost All Hallows Eve. He'd seen the gypsies going by in their rickety big wagons and as one went by the house the next day a big bale of hay fell off the back of their wagon. They went on, not knowing it happened. So the beekeeper got rabbit in her basket and went and picked up the bale of hay and took it off down the road after the gypsies, carrying it.

He was pretty far behind the gypsy caravan as they had already made camp; they had a big fire going already when he got there. They were so grateful and thankful to him for bringing them the bale of hay that they said, "Please stay for supper," and so he put his basket down next to him and decided to stay for dinner. When the gypsies saw the little rabbit and her big, beautiful blue eyes, they all stopped—silence was everywhere and everyone was looking at his rabbit.

Without a word, one of the elders went to the door of the big house wagon and rapped on it three times—knock, knock, knock. The door slowly opened. CREEEEEK. There stood a small, bent, ancient looking lady, the matriarch of the whole gypsy clan.

She stared, her eyes penetrating into and glaring at the rabbit, and then she spoke, holding one long, bent finger. "You have the enchanted one," she said, pointing at the blue eyed rabbit. "Be careful as there are those who would take her from you. She is only safe in your arms, especially at midnight on All Hallows Eve."

Why the man was suddenly frightened and didn't know what to do. He asked the old gypsy woman for her help or advice, anything. He so dearly loved the rabbit and didn't want any harm to come to her.

The old woman said to the beekeeper, "Get on your horse and ride to the end of your path and then ride back. Keep riding back and forth until the last stroke of midnight. Only then will she be safe from those who would snatch her!"

Shaken, our friend the beekeeper got the basket with his little rabbit in it, thanked them all for dinner, and, hurriedly, set off for home. The darkness of night started gathering in on them as the sun began to set.

When the beekeeper got home, he closed all the curtains and windows. Fall indeed was upon them and the chill of winter was coming. All Hallows Eve was approaching, too. He hadn't seen any of his bees for so long now and he missed them. Still, he would go each day and sit by their hives and talk to them. He just wanted to let them know that he was thinking of them, and of course, the blue-eyed rabbit would go, too.

October came and then week by week he waited and dreaded that night—All Hallows Eve. What if the scary old woman came to the house and was somehow able to get his rabbit? He just couldn't think of the possibilities. He decided that when the day and time came he would take the old gypsy woman's advice.

The day quickly approached. On All Hallows Eve, the entire village was celebrating with festivities in the marketplace. They were all having fun, but the beekeeper had long ago decided to stay home and follow the good advice he received from the gypsy woman. He put his dear sweet little rabbit in a special blanket, gathered her up close to his body, got on his horse, and then he rode for what seemed like hours on the road before his house. Down his path he went and up his path he went. Down his path he went and up his path he went—over and over again and again.

He was just about to give up and go in when he saw a dark and tricky looking shadow moving in the forest. He kept riding because he just knew who it was. It had to be that evil old woman. Without even having to look at his pocket watch, he could feel that the midnight hour was almost upon them. The beekeeper held his little rabbit closely and tightly to his body as the horse plodded on, almost on its own—down the path and up the path. Down the path and up the path.

Suddenly, the beekeeper heard the clock chime off in the village. It was very distant, but he heard it start chiming out the hour of midnight. Bong-bong-ding-dong-ding-dong-bong-ding-dong -ding dong-bong.

A wave of fear washed up over the beekeeper and he was clutching at his little rabbit so tightly now he was scared that he was going to hurt her. That's when he felt the wind picking up fast and hard. It was whipping all around him just like he was in the center of a tornado. The moon went behind a big, black cloud and our friend the beekeeper shivered with dread as he held tight to the little rabbit. He held onto her even when the ground shook underneath his horse's feet, scaring the animal something terrible. He could see his house and it was shaking too, as if

Why did this old woman want the man's rabbit?
Was a curse broken on All Hallow's Eve?

an earthquake came while they were riding by. He closed his eyes tightly against this evil and magical storm and began to pray.

Suddenly—it was all calm again and the whole area was deathly silent. It was as if they were in the eye of a hurricane. The beekeeper sat there upon his horse dazed and unable to move for many, many long moments. He was so beside himself he didn't even notice that his arms were no longer around his little rabbit. When he regained his senses and opened his eyes, he saw that the moon had come back out. It shone down on them like a beacon of light. It was then and there that the beekeeper noticed that in his arms was not a rabbit, but a beautiful blue-eyed, blond-haired young woman.

Indeed an enchantment had been broken.

The beekeeper and the lovely woman were married the next Sunday in the village. He brought honey and beeswax for everyone and all who attended the happy event rejoiced in the day.

From then on, when she would go to market with her husband the beekeeper, she would always have her arm around him. Everyone liked his new wife a great deal; she was so beautiful and so friendly. When the happy couple went to visit the gypsies, they were delighted with her, too.

One morning after church one of the fellows said to the beekeeper, "You know it's very strange, but no one has seen that creepy old woman around."

The beekeeper had asked about her last week and no one had seen her, but this fellow talked on a little and elaborated a bit. He said, "You know it's very curious, but the last time someone saw that scary old woman it was on All Hallows Eve. I remember it well, as we were all at the bonfire and we saw her, that old witch, going as fast as she could hobble down through the fields and then she disappeared at the edge of the river. We went down to rescue her, but she wasn't in need of rescue as she wasn't drowning. In fact, she wasn't there at all. It was very odd indeed." The fellow paused for a moment and took a few steps closer to the beekeeper. When he continued on with his story, he did so in almost a whisper. "But what was even odder was that we all saw a huge black cloud of bees that night—and they were chasing her down the road towards the river. And that's weird because everyone knows that bees don't come out in the winter. Not even your family of bees comes out in the cold months. Very strange indeed."

Our friend the beekeeper just smiled and hugged his beautiful, blue-eyed wife and said, "Yes, it's very strange indeed."

Oven Baked Southern Fried Honey Chicken

Ingredients:

3 to 4 pounds of chicken

1 teaspoon of paprika

1 cup of milk

1 cup flour

1/2 stick of melted butter

2 tablespoons of salt

2 tablespoons of garlic powder

1/4 teaspoon pepper

1 cup of chopped pecans

plenty of honey

Directions:

Pre-heat oven to 425 degrees Fahrenheit

Pour the butter in a foil lined baking dish

In a small brown paper bag, put in the paprika, flour, salt, garlic powder, and pepper; then shake up to mix well

Cut the chicken up and soak the pieces in the milk

Put chicken pieces one at a time in the bag, shaking to coat them well

Then place each coated piece in baking dish

Bake the chicken in the oven for 45 minutes

Remove, and while it's still sort of hot, drizzle honey all over the chicken; then, sprinkle with lots of pecans

Hoe Cakes

Ingredients:

- 1 cup corn meal
- 3/4 cup of boiling water
- 1 teaspoon of salt
- 1 tablespoon of butter or oil

Directions:

Pre-heat oven to 350 degrees Fahrenheit

Combine the meal and salt, then gradually add the water

Pour into the greased baking dish or a cast iron skillet, one that is at least an inch thick

Bake for 50-60 minutes or until it has a rich, brown, crunchy crust

Dip in honey or serve drizzled with warm honey

*If you try this recipe and decide that you'd rather have a cake that rises like corn bread,
then just add 2 teaspoons of baking powder to the batter*

Notes from Cyn:

The origins of this heart-warming story are Irish and it was brought to America when my ancestors came and settled here. These are two of my well-loved honey recipes, both of which happen to be Southern!

Back in the 1960s, my brother kept a beehive in our backyard. My brother and our father, Mack, dressed in bee keeper protective clothing while they enjoyed taking care of the hive. As they tended to the bees they, harvested honey and beeswax. The beeswax was great for making candles, which our family had a fun time doing. I molded it into shapes so we'd have them for German style Christmas ornaments as a memory of my Father. All these years later, I still have a piece of their beeswax.

Beeswax candles have been made for centuries and are important in many cultures even today. Honey has also been used for healing purposes since primitive times. It is soothing for colds and sore throats. Some entertainers insist on honey to eat as their "warm up" ritual for their voices. No wonder, since it is so delicious!

In olden days hoe cakes would have been baked in a wood stove or fried on a griddle with grease. They were called "hoe" cakes because they could be cooked on the farmer's hoe over a fire for a quick lunch when out in the field. In New England, hoe cakes were known as "Johnny cakes" and were also a diet staple that dates back all the way to the very first Thanksgiving.

11 | MAGIC FISH

Traditional Japanese Tale and Recipe for Baked and Stuffed Flounder

The fisherman and his wife lived at the edge of the sea in a small house. Each morning he would go out, cast his nets into the sea, and when he pulled them in they would be full of beautiful, flashy fish. One day when he threw his net out and pulled it back in he drew up in his nets a spectacularly beautiful fish. It stood on its tail and shimmered radiantly in the light—and then much to the fisherman's surprise, the fish began to speak to him in a sing-song manner.

"I am a magic fish... Cast me loose and I'll grant you a wish."

Well, the fisherman was so startled that he dropped the net and said, "Of course, go free." So the fish hopped out of the net and into the water and—splish splash—swam away.

The next day, the same thing happened again to the fisherman. He threw his nets out into the water and when he pulled them back in the boat there was the magic fish. Once again it said to him in its sing-song way of speaking: "I am a magic fish... Cast me loose and I'll grant you a wish."

The fisherman was less startled this time, but he knew that he had to free the fish. "Of course, go free." So the fish hopped out of the net and into the water and—splish splash—was about to swim away when it stopped and said to the fisherman, "What is your wish?"

The man thought, "Wish? Wish? I have everything I need; I have a house and a wife I love. Oh, I don't need a wish."

So the fish being very pleased—splish splash—swam away.

When he went home that night to tell his wife what had happened, oh she was furious with him. She said, "How could you not ask for your wish? Here we are living in this hovel of a shack with nothing good to eat and nothing proper to wear. Go back and ask that fish for all the money that will fit on the shore."

The next day the man did as his wife bade. He reluctantly threw his nets out into the water and when he pulled them back in the boat, lo and behold, there was the magic fish again. Once again the fish said to him in his song-like way: "I am a magic fish... Cast me loose and I'll grant you a wish."

The man felt very humble and finally said, "I hate to ask, but my wife... She would like a little more money. She asked me to ask you if we could not have a big pile of gold coins."

The fish regarded the man and nodded once. Then it said, "It is so, go home," and with that—splish splash—it swam away.

Well, the man hurried home to see how happy his wife would be with him and their new lot in life. To his surprise, there by his small little house was a huge pile of gold and coins. His wife was dancing around and throwing up the coins in the air. She lost no time in telling all of their friends of their sudden windfall. She went to town and began spending and spending and spending. Before the fisherman knew it, they had everything the market sold, more than they needed; in fact, they had two and three of everything.

Still, the wife was not content. She said to her husband the fisherman, "Go fishing tomorrow and get that fish back in the net. I want a grand mansion, the biggest and best house in the whole area."

Well, now the man thought to himself, "This will not end well." He loved his wife, but this just didn't seem right. Nevertheless, he went to the sea the next day like his wife bade him to do and went fishing just as he always did.

With a heavy heart, he threw his nets out into the water and when he pulled them back in the boat, lo and behold, there was the magic fish yet again. It was still a beautiful thing to see, but somehow it did not look as lovely as it did the very first time the fisherman had seen it. The fish said to the fisherman in his song-like way of speaking: "I am a magic fish... Cast me loose and I'll grant you a wish."

The fisherman was almost too ashamed to speak, but somehow he managed. "I'm sorry to ask, but it's my wife... She would like a big fabulous mansion for us to live in."

The fish paused for a moment regarding the fisherman. Then it finally spoke saying, "It is so, go home," and with that—splish splash—it swam away.

When the fisherman got home, there in front of what used to be their small little hovel was a huge, beautiful, fancy mansion. There was room after room, each filled with glorious furniture. People were coming by and looking at it and talking about it. The house was simply fabulous and for a while his wife seemed pleased, but the man just shook his head.

That night, when the husband and wife went to go to sleep, just as he put his head down upon the pillow, he said, "Well, I guess we finally have enough."

"Yes," agreed the wife, "but I was thinking..."

Sadly, the fisherman went to the sea the next day like his wife bade him to do and he went fishing just as he always did.

Paying little mind to what he did, he threw his nets out into the water and when he pulled them back in the boat, lo and behold, there was the magic fish again. It was still beautiful, but it most certainly did not look as exquisite as it did even the last time that fisherman had seen it. The fish said to the fisherman in his song-like way of speaking: "I am a magic fish... Cast me loose, and I'll grant you a wish."

So the fisherman asked the fish for a staff of servants to take care of everything, and her wish was granted, but still his wife demanded more.

The day after that she wanted coaches and carriages. The fisherman went out and asked this wish for her.

The day after that she wanted to have her own chapel. The fisherman went out and asked this wish for her, too.

Soon everyone in the land was talking about her. The man was very embarrassed. He didn't go fishing for several days and when she noticed that she pushed him down toward the docks and said, "This time when you catch that fish, I think I want to be queen of the world."

The husband sighed and shook his head. "Oh no! Queen of the world? Why would you want to be queen of the world? We have everything."

"Yes, I know," she said. "Now I want to be queen of the world." She forced him to go fishing again that day and once again he caught the magic fish. However, it was not quite as eager to see the fisherman this time—maybe because the fish did not look so well at all. Its beautiful iridescent scales were dull and, when it spoke his usual words to the fisherman, it did not do so with nearly the energy it used to have. The man was so deeply ashamed for himself, but he managed to say, "I hate to ask you, but my wife... She wants to be queen of the world."

This magic fish grew weary of the
wishes requested of him.

The fish sighed heavily and said, "It is so. Go home." With that—splish splash—it swam away.

When the fisherman got home, there indeed was his wife with a crown on her head and a whole lot of subjects milling around and bowing to her. She was just thrilled and delighted.

Till a few days later that is.

As she put her head on the pillow that night to go to sleep, she said to her husband, "You know dear, I wish I was the ruler of the universe."

"What!" said the husband. "The universe? No, we have everything. I am not asking that of the magic fish." The fisherman turned off the light and, rolling over, went to sleep.

Oh, that wife! She made the fisherman's life miserable. Day after day she badgered him and hounded him and annoyed him until it was all he could stand. He went and got into his boat and went fishing.

This time the fish was very slow in coming up to the surface. It didn't shimmer as much as it did even the last time he had seen it. All of its scales were completely dull and the fish itself was fairly listless. Mortified, the man said to the fish, "My wife... it's my wife. She is just completely out of control. Now, she wants to be ruler of the universe."

The fish hesitated this time and paused, letting his dull eyes regard the man before he said, "Go home... You will have what you deserve," and with that—splish splash—it swam away.

The fisherman went home very, very slowly; very, very reluctantly; and with a heavy, heavy heart. He was so sorry that he had let his wife tell him to do all this. He decided that he was going to put his principles first and not let her bully him into more wishes.

However, when he got back to what used to be the fine palatial estate they had been living in, there sat his wife, on a tree stump. Gone was the pile of gold. None of her many servants were around, the huge gold encrusted mansion was gone, so were the carriages and the custom built chapel, even the crown was missing from her head. The fisherman's wife was crying because everything that she had wished for was gone. Everything was back as it was and, except for their tiny little cottage, the beach was deserted.

The fisherman didn't even have to ask; he knew what had happened. When he went to her where she sat weeping on the tree stump, still loving her, he held her in his arms and comforted her. He said to her, "You'll see, we'll be just fine because we had everything that we needed long before we had everything that you wanted."

Baked And Stuffed Flounder

Ingredients:

1 very fresh, large cleaned flounder (If you are having company you can do 2 medium fish)

The fish should have the head still intact but if you have to you can use headless ones. Ask your fisherman to slit the fish on its edge to make a space for the stuffing

1/2 cup of olive oil

Sea salt, to taste

1 to 1-1/2 cups of store bought herb stuffing mix (or you can make your favorite bread and herb stuffing from scratch). The size of the fish determines the amount of stuffing. If you make too much stuffing, you can bake it separately.

1 can of well drained crab meat

2 to 3 tablespoons of garlic

2 to 3 tablespoons of rosemary

1 to 2 tablespoons of thyme

3 or 4 tablespoons of parsley

Directions:

Pre-heat oven to 350 degrees Fahrenheit

If your fish is uncut, with a sharp knife, cut a slit in the fish to hold the stuffing

Follow the directions for making the stuffing: the consistency should be moist, but not too watery; then add the crab meat and set aside until needed

Oil the top, bottom, and inside of your fish

Sprinkle and rub all the herbs on the top, bottom, and inside of the fish

Put the stuffing in the cavity of the fish and gently close it shut

Lay the fish in a foil lined baking dish

Bake for 25 to 30 minutes or until the fish is flaky

Notes from Cyn:

This folktale can be found in different versions from many cultures. One of my favorites is from Japan, an old country with many fish and sea stories. This is also a favorite with storytelling audiences of all ages.

I began teaching the art of Gyutaku, or Japanese fish printing, when I could add an activity to a program with this story and in my art classes. This old art form was begun by Japanese fishermen as a record-keeping method, as they often recorded the size and types of the fish they caught.

Originally it was made using India ink painted on a real fish and then a piece of rice paper was pressed onto the fish to make a print. Once dry, it became a beautiful piece of artwork. Later artists used color paint and printing ink and regular but thin paper. I also printed fish on textiles with good results. The problem with doing Guytaku for a week with seven hundred elementary students is that you need fresh fish. I solved that by putting the fish in the teacher's staff lounge refrigerator until I had to stop because everyone complained about the "fishy" smell in the front hall of Summerfield School. It also meant you couldn't serve the fish for dinner after 702 printings!

12 | TOO MUCH NOISE

A Russian Tale with the Recipe for Mother Moore's Meatloaf

Once upon a time, a man and his wife lived in their charming but small house with their three children, their dog, and their cat. They had a wonderful life, filled with love and laughter. One day when the man got home from work the little house just seemed to be so noisy. The roof was leaking—drip, drip, drip; the faucet was running—swoosh, swoosh, swoosh; the baby was crying—wha, wha, wha; the dog was barking—woof, woof, woof; the children were bickering—nay, nay, nay; the cat was mewing—meow, meow, meow. There was just too much noise. He held his ears, screamed, and ran out the door.

He decided to go down to the village and ask the Wiseman what he should do. The Wiseman said, "Get a cow."

"A cow?" he thought. "What good is a cow going to do? Besides, my wife will not let me bring a cow into the house." However, he went home and did as the wise man said.

So that meant the roof was leaking—drip, drip, drip; the faucet was running—swoosh, swoosh, swoosh; the baby was crying—wha, wha, wha; the dog was barking—woof, woof, woof; the children were bickering—nay, nay, nay; the cat was mewing—meow, meow, meow; and now a cow was mooing—moo, moo, moo. He put his hands over his ears and went screaming from the house, "There is too much noise!"

The husband went down again to the village to consult the Wiseman. The Wiseman told him get some chickens.

The man went and got some chickens as he was advised by the Wiseman. Against his wife's wishes, he took them into the house.

Now the roof was leaking—drip, drip, drip; the faucet was running—swoosh, swoosh, swoosh; the baby was crying—wha, wha, wha; the dog was barking—woof, woof, woof; the children were bickering—nay, nay, nay; the cat was mewing—meow, meow, meow; the cow was mooing—moo, moo, moo; and now the chickens were clucking—cluck, cluck, cluck. Of course the man couldn't stand it; he clapped his hands over his ears and ran from the house screaming, "There's too much noise!"

The husband ran back to the Wiseman and this time the Wiseman said, "Get a Billy-goat."

Not understanding why, the man did as he was advised. He went home and pulled a Billy-goat into the house. By now you can imagine the cute little house was very, very crowded and all the while the roof was leaking—drip, drip, drip; the faucet was running—swoosh, swoosh, swoosh; the baby was crying—wha, wha, wha; the dog was barking—woof, woof, woof; the children were bickering—nay, nay, nay; the cat was mewing—meow, meow, meow; the cow was mooing—moo, moo, moo; the chickens were clucking—cluck, cluck, cluck; and now the Billy-goat was bleating—baa, baa, baa. The man clapped his hands over his ears and ran from the house screaming, "There's TOO MUCH NOISE!"

The next morning, having gotten no sleep at all, the man was groggy as he went down to the village, making his way very slowly as he traveled. He went to the Wiseman and said, "What can I do? It is getting worse and worse."

The Wiseman just smiled and said to the husband, "Get rid of the goat. Get rid of the chickens. Get rid of the cow." Well, the man turned right back around and made his way home. Before he went to bed that night, he did as the Wiseman said and took the goat, chickens, and cow all outside. When he came back into his little house and listened, the roof was still leaking—drip, drip, drip; the faucet was still running—swoosh, swoosh, swoosh; the baby was still crying—wha, wha, wha; the dog was still barking—woof, woof, woof; the children were still bickering—nay, nay, nay; and the cat was still mewing—meow, meow, meow...but you know what? It was not too much noise after all; it was just a happy home.

'...the roof was leaking—drip, drip, drip; the faucet was running—swoosh, swoosh, swoosh; the baby was crying—wha, wha, wha; the dog was barking—woof, woof, woof; the children were bickering—nay, nay, nay; the cat was mewing—meow, meow, meow; the cow was mooing—moo, moo, moo; the chickens were clucking—cluck, cluck, cluck; and now the Billy-goat was bleating—baa, baa, baa." It was enough to drive one husband and father almost insane.

Mother Moore's Meatloaf

Ingredients

1-1/2 to 2 pounds of good ground beef

3 slices of bread

1 minced onion

3/4 cup of ketchup

1 tablespoon of Worcestershire sauce

1 egg

1 teaspoon of salt

1/4 teaspoon of pepper

1 eight ounce can of diced tomatoes

1 four ounce can of sliced mushrooms

1 green pepper, chopped

Directions:

Preheat oven to 350 Fahrenheit

Using your hands, mix all the ingredients together in a large bowl, but add the meat last and slowly

Place the mixture in a well greased loaf pan, about an 8 x 12 inch. If you don't have one this big then shape the mixture into a loaf and use a large baking dish

Bake for an hour

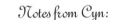

Notes from Cyn:

We call them comfort food in this modern day and age. Mashed potatoes, macaroni and cheese, both of these are warm and homey; they're more popular now than ever before. Meatloaf was a favorite with 1950s American families. Back then, our family ate it with mashed or baked potatoes and some green vegetables. It's interesting that it is continuing on in our modern times as a "comfort food." You can even find it now on upscale restaurant menus, so there again—food defines the era with the family bonds being a soothing, safe reminder. The smells in the kitchen and eating these favorites bring back memories of a simpler, safer life.

13 | SILLY JACK

A North Carolina Mountains tale with Recipes for Aunt Becky's Banana Pudding & Addie Mae's Cherry Pie

Jack and his mamma were doing just fine, thank you very much. The neighbors all took care of each other back then like they should even now.

One morning Jack's mamma woke up and said, "You know Jack, I think that Farmer Lilly needs some help today. I want you to go on up there and give him some help around the farm."

"Yes mama," said Jack.

Mamma gave him a little lunch, kissed him, and sent him off.

Jack enjoyed himself. He liked doing things around the farm and helping folks out like Farmer Lilly. Farmer Lilly was a nice man who was teaching Jack some stuff, too. That night when it was time for Jack to go home Farmer Lilly's wife said, "Jack, we just appreciate so much everything you did around here today and coming to help us I want to send this home with you honey child. It's a nice fresh loaf of home-baked bread. I know your mamma likes this kind."

Farmer Lilly's wife gave him the bread and Jack took off for home just a-singing and a-dancing as he went. Not wanting to drop the bread, Jack grabbed it up and held onto it tight, digging his fingers deep, deep, deep into the loaf and scrunching it up into his fist.

When Jack got home, his mamma said, "Jack, honey, what is this you have in your fist?"

"It's a loaf of bread, mamma... Farmer Lilly's wife gave it to me for us to eat," said Jack.

"But it's gotten holes all in it and is scrunched up here in the middle, we can't eat this now," said Jack's mamma. "Didn't I ever tell you the proper way to carry home a loaf of bread?"

Jack shook his head and said, "No, mamma, you never have."

"Well, you go and get some great big leaves and wrap it up all careful like," she said, "and then you place it in your hat and put your hat on your head. Then you come home straight away, no singing and dancing."

"All right mamma, I'll do that next time," said Jack happy that he had learned something useful.

The next day mamma woke up Jack bright and early and sent him back to work on Farmer Lilly's farm. She packed him a lunch, kissed him on the top of his head, and said to him, "Now, you be a good boy Jack, and remember what I said."

"I will mamma," and Jack went on up the road up to Farmer Lilly's place. After a full day of work, the farmer's wife called Jack over to her and said, "Now, Jack, you just worked as hard as you could all day long, I want to send you home with a little something special. Here, take this ball of butter I freshly churned today... Give it to your mamma."

"Thank you, I will," said Jack. He took the butter and started on home, but before he got too far, Jack remembered what his mamma said. He looked around, found some large leaves, wrapped up the butter carefully and placed it in his hat. The he put the hat on his head and began the long walk home without singing or dancing. Soon Jack grew hot and that butter on top of his head began to melt and run down all over him.

By the time he arrived home, it had melted away down to nothing. He had butter all down his neck, back, chest, and arms. His mamma took one look at him and said, "Jack, what is that all over you?"

"Melted butter," Jack said.

"How on earth did you get melted butter all over you, Jack?" his mamma asked.

"I wrapped it up in leaves, put it in my hat, put my hat on my head and walked home without singing or dancing. I did just like you said to do mamma."

"Oh, Jack," mamma was sadly disappointed in her simple, silly son, but tried not show it. She knew she had to teach him better. "That is not how you carry butter. You take the butter down to the river and let it soak there until it gets good and cold. Then you carry it on back to the house without singing or dancing. Do you understand Jack?"

"Yes, mamma. I'll do better tomorrow," Jack said happy that he had learned something useful.

The next day Mamma woke up Jack bright and early and sent him back to work on Farmer Lilly's farm. She packed him a lunch, kissed him on the top of his head, and said to him, "Now, you be a good boy Jack, and remember what I said to you yesterday."

"I will, mamma," and Jack went on up the road up to Farmer Lilly's place. After a full day of work, the farmer's wife called Jack over to her and said, "Now,

Jack, you have been one of the best workers we've had in a long while. I want to give you something special. We have us here some puppies that are ready to go to good homes. I want you to pick one out and keep it for yourself."

Jack was delighted to have a dog all his own. He had always wanted his own doggie. They could play, have fun, and even sleep together. He went over and looked at all the little puppies and picked out the one that he liked the best. He thanked Farmer Lilly and his wife and began the trek home, but not too far down the road, Jack remembered what his mamma had told him yesterday. He took the puppy over to a stream and held it the water for a long, long, time, making sure that the puppy got good and wet and was shivering cold.

When he got home, his mamma said to him. "Jack, what do you have there?"

"It's a puppy, mamma. Farmer Lilly's wife gave it to me for all the hard work I've been doing for them." And he showed his mother the poor, shivering, water-logged puppy.

Mamma's heart just broke in two. She took up the puppy, quickly wrapping it in a warm towel. "Oh, Jack, how could you?" she said to her son. "This is a puppy, not a ball of butter—you could have drowned it."

"I'm sorry, mamma... I just did like you said to do."

"Yes, you did, but that is not how you take a puppy home. You get some string and tie it around its neck. The puppy will then follow you home. Do you understand now, Jack?"

"Yes mamma. I'll do better tomorrow," Jack said, happy that he had learned something useful.

The next day Mamma woke up Jack bright and early and sent him back to work one more time on Farmer Lilly's farm. She packed him a lunch, kissed him on the top of his head and said to him, "Now, Jack, please, please, please, you be a good boy and try real hard to remember what I said to you yesterday."

"I will, mamma," and Jack went on up the road up to Farmer Lilly's place. After his last full day of work up on the farm, the farmer's wife called Jack over to her and said, "Now, Jack, I made this special occasion cake just for you. It's a nice rich yellow cake with thick sweet icing. Take it on home with you, and make sure to thank your mamma for sending you up here to work for us all this week."

"I will, and thank you Mrs. Lilly," said Jack as he began his trip on home. But before he got too far down the road, he remembered what Mamma had said to him just yesterday. He dug through his pockets, found some string, and tied it very carefully around the cake. Then, placing the cake on the ground, he began to walk home just figuring that the cake was following behind.

When Mamma saw Jack coming up the walk, she began to grow a little anxious. As soon as he came in the house, she saw that he had something tied to a string, but could not make out what it was because it was covered with sticks, leaves, and dirt. "What do you have there, Jack?" she asked, almost afraid of what he may answer.

"It's a celebration cake, from Mrs. Lilly, for all the hard work I did. I tied it to a string and let it follow me home, just like you said mamma."

Mamma shook her head in disbelief at her poor, simple, silly son. She smiled wearily. Jack was listening, he just wasn't thinking. He was not going back to the Lilly's farm tomorrow, and no harm was done after all. She hugged him and sent him to wash up for supper. Unfortunately, they had no dessert that night.

"Jack," she said "I have to go out to the barn and bring in some milk so we can drink it with dinner."

"Alright mamma."

"But listen to me very carefully," she said to Jack as she stood at the door. "I worked hard all day making peach and apple pies. I laid them out on the back porch to cool. Please Jack, please, be very careful where you step."

"I will mamma."

Content, mamma went out the front door and off to the barn leaving Jack alone in the house. Jack stood there for a moment and thought very hard about what his mamma had said to him. She had told him to be very careful about stepping in those peach and apple pies. So Jack, not wanting to upset his mamma, opened up the back door and stood in front of those pies. They were all nicely lined up, one after another. Jack stood before the first pie, lifted his foot up high and was very careful about where he placed it back down—right in the middle of the first pie! Proud of what a good job he did, he moved onto the second pie. Then the third, and then the fourth, and so on down the line.

Well... No dessert again that evening. Besides that, Jack got a good scrubbing and talkin' to. Far as I know, folks are still telling Silly Jack's tale. Guess they hope their children and friends will learn a little something. Then maybe there will be dessert after dinner.

Sweet, silly Jack tried so hard to do
as his Momma taught him...

Aunt Becky's Banana Pudding

Ingredients:

2 boxes of vanilla pudding

Milk for the pudding according to the directions on the box (you can make pudding with your favorite pudding recipe instead of course)

1 cup of sour cream

1 box of vanilla wafers

2 small containers of a whipped cream dessert topping or real whipping cream whipped stiff

3 or 4 ripe bananas, sliced

Directions:

Line a baking dish with vanilla wafers and add a row around the edges

Layer banana slices on top of them.

Prepare the pudding according to the directions

Mix the sour cream into the cooled pudding

Next, fold in the whipped cream dessert topping or your own whipped cream, reserving some for the top

Pour 1/2 the pudding mixture on top of your layers

Make another layer of vanilla wafers and cookies and bananas

Layer the rest of the pudding on top

Top with your remaining whipped cream

Place in the refrigerator and let it chill for 2 to 3 hours before you enjoy!

Notes from Cyn:

Aunt Becky Leonard is no longer with us, but her delicious banana pudding, like a good folk tale, has been passed down from our family to yours. Becky's Banana Pudding is a family favorite we still make. The next generation has tangible family history. Our great nieces are trying it now as babies. We will all be making this recipe and telling tales about the lovely Aunt Becky and the funny Silly Jack for many more years to come. It is a favorite with our friends and neighbors who enjoyed it for many years at our celebrations.

This story of Silly Jack is another one that can be heard in other countries with variations. I heard it as an African folktale years before I heard it as a Southern tale. The sequencing and variety of food carried home was changed, but the ideas were the same.

Addie Mae's Famous "Cherry Pie"

Pie Filling

Ingredients:

- 1 can sweetened condensed milk (8 oz)
- 1 teaspoon of vanilla extract
- 1/3 cup of lemon juice
- 8 oz Philadelphia Cream Cheese softened
- 1/2 cup of heavy whipping cream beaten until it's stiff
- 1 pie shell or a graham cracker crust pie shell

Directions:

Mix the sweetened condensed milk, the vanilla extract, the soft cream cheese, and the lemon juice together

Then, fold in the whipped cream

Pour it all into the prepared pie shell

Place in the refrigerator and let it chill for 2 to 3 hours before you enjoy!

Pie Topping

Ingredients:

- 1 can tart cherries, drained but save the juice
- 1 tablespoon of corn starch
- 1/4 cup of sugar
- Red food coloring

Directions:

Under a low flame, heat the juice, cornstarch, and sugar until it thickens

Add the cherries

What you'll have now will be a shade of pink, so carefully add a drop of red food coloring, one at a time, until you have a shade of red that you like

Let the topping cool

Carefully, pour the topping over the cream mixture in the pie shell

Cool in the refrigerator for at least 2 hours before serving

Notes from Cyn:

My husband's mother, Addie Mae, has been making this delicious cherry pie for five decades. It is similar to cheese cake but with a softer pudding filling. Cherry pie is the most often requested dessert by everyone in the family for birthdays, parties, and plain old dinner dessert. Mom's cherry pie and Aunt Becky's banana pudding have also been the stars of our big pig pickin' barbecues for hundreds of our friends, family, and neighbors down through the years. The pudding and pie pans are always sent home empty.

14 | NANNY GOAT & HER TWO KIDS

A Cautionary Tale with a Recipe for Dilly Bread

There once was a sweet mother goat, a nanny goat, who lived with her two dear sons, Peter and Paul, in a small cave in the forest at the edge of the mountains. Each day she would go and find food for her children and take it back with her for them to eat. As the boys grew older they stopped staying home while she foraged and went out and helped her.

One day she had heard that the big mean old bear had been around. She said to her sons, "My dears, you must stay home today because if the bear were to come upon us he would eat you up in one bite and I would not be able to save you. So, close and lock the door behind me after I leave and don't let anyone in."

"Yes mamma," said Peter.

"Yes mamma," said Paul.

With that, our mamma nanny goat went out to forage and find food for her two sons.

Well, she hadn't been gone for very long when the two little billy goats heard a KNOCK KNOCK KNOCK at the door.

Peter ran up to the door and said, "Who is it?"

Paul ran up next to his brother.

Together they heard a little voice say, "It's me, your mother, let me back in for I have come home."

Well, Paul, being the smarter of the two brothers, pulled aside the curtain and there outside the door he saw the biggest, blackest, meanest looking bear he had ever seen. He let the curtain fall back and yelled out, "Go away, go away! We don't want to let you in, bear!"

The bear turned and left in disgust at those smart billy goats.

Well, it hadn't been too much longer after that when they heard a SCRATCH SCRATCH SCRATCH at the door.

Peter ran up to the door and said, "Who is it?"

Paul ran up next to his brother once again.

Together they heard the same sweet voice from before, but this time it said, "It's I, your dear mamma. I've come back with some food... Let me in."

Then, the little billy goats saw beautiful red fingernails poke out from underneath the door—seemingly like the kind their mother wore—but they ran to the window and, pulling back the curtain, took a peek outside. There by the door they saw that big, huge, mean, black grizzly bear pretending to be their mother again. The bear had crushed red berries on his claws to make them look pretty like Mother Goat.

The big, huge, mean black bear was determined to get his meal—even if he had to pretend to be their mother.

So they let the curtain fall back and yelled out together, "Go away, bear, go away! We don't want to let you in! You're not our mother! We can tell, your voice is not right, you don't sound like her."

The bear stomped away disgusted. Getting dinner had never been this hard before. He went off into the woods and drank a whole lot of honey and then he practiced pretending to be the mamma nanny goat.

"Hello?" he tried in a little voice. And then drank some honey.

"Hello?" he tried in a higher pitched voice. And then he drank some more honey.

"Hello!" He tried in yet another voice. And then he drank even more honey.

Sure enough drinking all that honey had made his voice sound soft and sweet and loving sounding. He sounded just like the mamma nanny goat.

Now the bear went back to the little cave house in the woods near the base of the mountains. He gently placed his big paw on the door and SCRATCH SCRATCH SCRATCH.

Peter ran up to the door and said, "Who is it?"

Paul came and ran up next to his brother.

Together they heard a sweet and melodious voice say, "It's I, your dear mamma."

The brothers ran to the window and pulled the curtain back, taking a peek outside. This time, though, they didn't see the bear—in fact, they didn't see anyone standing there.

Peter said, "Let's open the door. I'm hungry."

Paul shook his head no and replied, "No, I don't think we should. It might be mamma, but it could be a trick of that old bear."

"No," said Peter, "It couldn't be."

With that said, he flung open the door—and there stood that huge, giant, big black grizzly bear. He roared and charged into the house. He chased those two billy goats all around the cave. He ate up Peter—GULP!—just like that in one bite...and then he ate the other brother, Paul—GULP!—just like that in one bite also.

With his meal complete, the bear left the cave and went back to his place in the woods to take a little nap.

When mamma nanny goat came home and drew close to her cave, she grew suddenly cautious. The front door was standing wide open. She was worried. As she carefully moved closer, she saw that her home was ransacked and her two beloved sons were missing. She instantly knew that somehow that big, black, mean grizzly bear had eaten up her boys.

"Oh dear!" she thought to herself. "The worst has happened! What am I going to do?" As she sat there crying, she formulated a cunning plan.

Underneath the cave was a root cellar where the mamma nanny goat stored her vegetables and kept her extra things, so she opened the door to it and over the top she carefully laid soft pine branches making a nice big, comfy pile of them.

She finished and just in the nick of time too, as she heard the big, black bear coming this way as he crashed through the forest.

As the bear stood in the door of her home, she could tell that he was ready to open up his mouth and eat her up just like he had done to her boys, but the mamma nanny goat was too quick. She stopped him and said, "Wait! I was just about to make some supper. Would you like to stay? I'm making a delicious, delicious stew."

The bear, always hungry, and always loving home-cooked food, said okay and accepted mamma nanny goat's offer. He watched her cook as she stirred and stirred the ingredients in her cooking pot.

"You're looking a bit tired," mamma nanny goat said. "Would you like to sit and rest for a while on my lovely couch of pine branches?"

The bear paused. He watched her as the steam from the pot was rising and smelling so good. It was so delicious smelling that it momentarily took his mind away from anything logical. He turned and sat down on the pine branches.

There was a loud CRASH! as he fell all the way down the hole and into the root cellar. When he opened his mouth to roar up in anger at the mamma nanny goat—ROAR!—out jumped Peter, out jumped Paul, and they both ran straight over to their mamma. They were both just fine.

Mamma quickly closed the door and locked that big old mean bear in the root cellar. She kept him in there until he made her a solemn promise that he would never come calling on them again. Once he did—and Mamma nanny goat believed him—she opened the root cellar door, letting the big, black grizzly bear go free.

You should have seen just how fast that bear ran out of there, like a shot he went—WOOSH! He was not about to stay one minute longer than he had to with someone as smart as the mamma nanny goat.

So it was from then on the little billy goats knew not to ever open the door to a stranger, even if they did have red toenails and a honey soft voice like their mamma's.

Dilly Bread

Ingredients:

- 1/4 cup of warm water
- 1 package of yeast
- 1 egg
- 1 cup of cottage cheese
- 2 tablespoons of minced onion
- 1 tablespoon of melted butter
- 2 tablespoons of sugar
- 1 teaspoon of salt
- 1/4 teaspoon of baking soda
- 1 tablespoon of dried dill or 1 1/2 tablespoons of fresh dill (not both)
- 2-1/2 cups of flour

Directions:

Preheat oven to 350 Fahrenheit

In a small bowl, dissolve the yeast in the warm water

In a large bowl, combine the cottage cheese and butter and stir until just blended

Slowly add the egg, onion, sugar, salt, baking soda, dill seed, and yeast mixture. Stir until well blended.

Add the flour and stir well

Cover the mixture with a damp cloth and let the dough rise until it doubles in size, this should take about 1 to 1-1/2 hours

Punch the dough down and put in a greased loaf pan

Cover and let rise 40-50 minutes

Bake for 50-60 minutes

Remove from oven and brush the top with melted butter

Notes from Cyn:

We lived in a one hundred-year-old log cabin on Horsepen Creek Road for three years. It was the late 1970s and a fun time of my life. I cooked and baked a lot there enjoying the simple life and foods. Why? It felt good to be making our meals with my own hands. I began my herb growing and gardening there for the first time. I felt like an "earth mother," you know someone who lives the simple life by living close to the land. Eventually, we moved back to town with a faster paced life. It would be years until I had the time to bake bread and grow herbs again. It was an empty spot in my life that I happily now again fill with good food and good times with friends and family. My flower garden and herbs are a peaceful sanctuary especially in the spring, summer, and fall.

15 | JACK AND THE ROBBERS

A Centuries-old Folktale and a Recipe for Grandma Brown's Corn Pudding and Chocolate Pound Cake

This tale is an old one, probably first told by the Bremen town musicians. Many centuries ago folk tales were passed down and carried across the ocean when people emigrated from their native countries in Europe and settled in America. They brought more than their children, trunks, and pets—they also brought with them their stories.

Jack lived in the mountains, in one of the hollers, with his family. He was a good boy, and he and his brothers and sisters, all ten of them, tried to help out on the farm. One day, why, he was a bit lazy and it was his turn to chop firewood. They heated their house with it and needed it for everyday cooking so someone always had to chop and chop to make sure that they always had enough wood piled up. This was a chore that had to be done every day, all year round, so that the family could make sure that they had plenty of wood piled up for the cold, cold winters in the North Carolina Mountains. The snow piled up to the eaves of the roof sometimes and you had to keep a fire going to keep the house warm.

For Jack, though, it was the lazy time of summer and he was enjoying himself just rocking in his hammock, and playing with his dogs and petting on his kitty cat that was sitting on his lap. Jack just did not want to get up and sweat and chop wood. Maybe one of his brothers would want to do it, or at least, do it for him. He planned on staying right where he was.

Well, the brothers wanted to lollygag around also, which meant that the firewood did not get cut. When Daddy came in from the fields, he was furious. "What are these logs just a-sitting here and not cut?" he demanded to know. "You boys all know that we have got to keep up with chopping firewood so that we'll have enough for the winter. Why it could turn cold early. Come on, get out there Jack and get to chopping, it's your turn."

Jack complained the whole way over to the logs. He thought that his daddy just didn't understand that boys liked to fool about in the summer time. Besides, it was almost supper time and he was hungry. Mamma was fixing it right now and he could smell her good cooking, her fried chicken. He was hoping that she'd make his favorite corn pudding. She made it most times because the harvest had been so good, especially with the corn. That's why they had it most every evening.

Jack sat himself down on the log and was sniffing at his supper. He let himself get to day-dreaming again, that is, until Daddy came around.

"Jack," Daddy shouted at him, "are you still lollygagging around?" You could tell by his tone of his voice that he was not happy with his son. "I swear boy, you are just lazy. You go on and get up into that house. You get into your room and you stay there and there'll be no supper for you."

ARG! Jack was so mad! He was kicking at rocks in the dust as he went into the house. He tromped all the way through the house, glaring at every one of his brothers and sisters as he passed by. It was all their fault after all. One of them could have just gone and chopped that firewood if it was so important.

He climbed up the rungs of the ladder that led to his bedroom in the loft of the house. He lay down on his bed and fumed. He could hear everybody talking and having a good old time and eating all that delicious food Mamma made, especially that corn pudding. Oh, but his tummy growled with hunger and was hurting.

Jack got madder and madder and madder—and you know now, you should control your anger because if you don't it can get you into trouble. For Jack this was about to be one of those times.

Jack... He was so mad by the time that the house had quieted down. His brothers had come on up to bed, and all the other family members had also retired for the night. Once all the candles and lanterns had been extinguished, that's when he decided that he was going to run away.

That's right—Jack felt that running away would solve all his problems. He wouldn't have to do chores no more. He wouldn't have to worry about all those brothers and sisters getting everything. He was just gonna get himself on outta there, so very quietly as not to wake anybody, he climbed down the trellis on the side of their old pole cabin and crept away in the middle of the night.

Ah, he was free, FREE! He could do whatever he wanted to. He could be his own boss. He could set down his own rules. No more doing chores. He was just a-going down the road boggity-boggity, boggity- boggity, boggity-boggity, boggity! He hadn't gotten far when there in the middle of the road he saw a dog. It was a mangy, scrawny old dog just sitting there a-scratching at its fleas.

Jack said, "Whatcha you doin' there dog, sitting in the middle of the road in the middle of the night?"

The dog said, "Well, my master says that I'm too old and weak to scare away the foxes from the hen house. He's done put me out. Won't feed me no more."

So Jack said to the dog, "Well, I'm running away from home. Why dontcha come with me?"

The dog did and together they went on down the road boggity-boggity, boggity-boggity, boggity-boggity, boggity!

It was one of them moonless nights, nice and clear; lightning bugs about but no mosquitoes. As Jack and the dog were making their way down the old road, they saw up ahead of them a great big shadow.

When they got closer to it, they realized that it was he-haw, he-haw, he-haw an old donkey. He was grey all around his muzzle and just looked quite pitiful.

Jack said, "Whatcha you doin' there donkey, sitting in the middle of the road in the middle of the night?"

The donkey said, "Well, I've gotten too old to pull the plow. My master says that he can't feed mouths that don't work so he's gone and put me out."

So Jack said to the donkey, "Well, we're running away from home. Why dontcha come with us?"

The donkey did, and together they all went on down the road boggity-boggity, boggity-boggity, boggity-boggity, boggity!

It weren't all that long before Jack and the dog were riding up on top of that donkey, as it turned out that he had a little more fire left in him. Before long, however, they came upon a cat sitting there in the middle of the road.

Jack said, "Whatcha you doin' there cat, sitting in the middle of the road in the middle of the night?"

The cat said, "Well, I've gotten too old to catch the mice for my mistress like I'm supposed to, so she turned me out saying no more milk for me."

So Jack said to the cat "Well, we're running away from home. Why dontcha come with us?"

The cat did, and together they all went on down the road boggity-boggity, boggity-boggity, boggity-boggity, boggity!

They had just about gotten too tired to go on any further for the night when there in the middle of the road they saw a poor, sad looking rooster, barely able to crow.

Jack said, "Whatcha you doin' there rooster, sitting in the middle of the road in the middle of the night?"

The rooster says, "Well, I've gotten too old to be of any interest to the hens and I sleep past the rising of the sun. So because of that my master is going to put me in the pot and cook me for Sunday supper."

So Jack said to the rooster, "Well, we're running away from home. Why dontcha come with us?"

The rooster did, and together they all went on down the road boggity-boggity, boggity-boggity, boggity-boggity, boggity!

Now, they had been riding up there on the donkey for some time now, and it was very late. Everyone was tired and thirsty, but it was still night time and back in those days there were no big fancy hotels or motels where our friends could stop and get a room for the night. No, back then in the olden times you had to stay with somebody or hope that someone would take pity on a traveling stranger and let you sleep in their barn, so the group of them kept their eyes opened for someplace they could stay, but there was nothing anywhere to be seen. It was the most empty, desolate looking farmland any of them had ever been through.

The dog said in a hopeful tone, "We should be getting to a town soon, Jack."

Jack, though, was about to give up and sleep in the middle of the road himself — he was plum worn out and he was thirsty and tired and hungry to boot.

At just about that time, the rooster crowed and said that up ahead he saw a house. As they drew closer to it, they saw that there weren't any lights on and, as they drew even closer, Jack said, "Well, it looks like nobody lives here. This would be a good place for us to sleep." So they all went on up to it.

The grass was grown up and the windows were all cracked; the paint was all old and peeling. The garden was overrun with weeds. It looked like nobody had lived there in a very, very long time. This would be perfect for them, they thought. They figured that they could even stay there for a couple of days while they tried to figure out what they were going to do.

They pushed the door open. All of the animals and Jack went on inside—and it was then as they entered the front door that Jack smelled something wonderful.

Now the furniture was all old and broken, the fireplace was cold and dark, and there weren't any lanterns to light. He could just barely see anything at all, but Jack smelled fried chicken—and he smelled corn pudding. Oh, he started getting hungry.

"I smell us some supper! It must be around here somewhere," Jack threw open the door to the kitchen and Lawda Mercy, there was a whole big long trestle table full with a feast. There was a whole big turkey with all the trimmings. There were huge bowls of mashed potatoes; there were huge bowls of sweet peas, and there were huge baskets of big, fluffy biscuits. There were all kinds of delicious meats both baked and broiled, and corn pudding too; in fact, there were two different kinds. Then, then he saw the pies! The apple pie, the cherry pie, the peach pie, the persimmon pudding, and, lo and behold, his favorite dessert of all time—chocolate pound cake!

Jack and his newfound friends fell upon that feast and began eating, and eating, and eating. Everyone ate until they were full and could eat no more. Then the donkey had a thought. He said, "Jack, now wait a minute here. If this is one of them abandoned house that have been left by their family, then why is all this delicious fresh food here?"

Oh, no, they thought. The donkey had a point.

Jack stopped eating and with a heavy sigh, sat down in the rocking chair, and began thinking out loud. "An old abandoned house with supper ready and nobody home in the middle of the night in the middle of nowhere..."

"Oh no!" said the donkey. "I know what this is."

"What?" said Jack. "What? Quick tell us."

"Why, this has got to be one of them robber hide-outs," the donkey said. "You know, highway men who rob folks up and down the main road. I bet that here is where they hide out. Oh, Jack. I bet that they'll be coming home any minute! We are going to be in so much trouble if they catch us. We ate all their supper, they'll never forgive us. Besides, they're not going to like us knowing about this place. They can't take a chance that we may tell someone about it. We have got to get out of here now and fast."

With that Jack and all the animals started moving towards the front door to leave, but then—they heard somebody walking up the front steps. Thump, thump, thump, somebody with huge feet. Thump, thump, thump.

Jack peeked out the window and gasped at what he saw. "Oh, my gosh!" said Jack, nearly breathless with fear. "Y'all are not going to believe who is outside the door right now. It's Wild Hair Willy, the infamous robber and cut-throat thief. We gotta do something. There's a whole band of his robbers outside the door, too. Why, these cut-throat thieves are going to tear us limb from limb for using their house and eating their food! What are we going to do?"

Well, the donkey was the smartest of all of them and he was already thinking, thinking, thinking. In fact, he had been thinking hard and fast since he first figured out what kind of place this was. Then he said suddenly, "Jack, I know what we can do."

"Well hurry up and tell us!" Jack hollered back.

The donkey motioned for everyone to huddle up around him and he quickly whispered out his plan to his friends. Jack nodded his head in agreement. He liked the plan a lot. He and the animals knew just what to do... Now, here is what they did—just in case you find that you have to do this yourself one day.

Jack sat in the rocking chair, which he pulled back into the deep, dark shadows. The dog hid behind the door so that when it opened up, no one would see him when he'd spring out a-biting. The cat crawled in the fireplace. She had those long claws ready and a-waiting to strike. The rooster went up on top of the roof and perched on the chimney. The donkey carefully slipped out the back door and made his way around to the front.

Then they waited...and not a moment too soon either because with that POW! The front door flew open with a loud bang and there before their eyes stood in the doorway the tallest, the blackest shadow that they had ever seen and they all just knew who it was. Why, it was none other than Wild Hair Willy, the worst of the cut-throat robbers that there ever was.

Now in case you don't know, Wild Hair Willy was the meanest, the baddest, highwayman in those there parts at that time. He was said to be almost seven feet tall. He had a big bushy beard and a big bushy head of hair. He wore the oldest, nastiest clothes that he could find. Why he smelled so bad that he stunk to high heaven. He never took a bath, he never brushed his teeth. Wild Hair Willy was the leader of the merciless robber band and he was coming in the front door.

Jack's knees were a-knocking, he was so scared. He was afraid that Willy would hear him. The animals were so quiet you couldn't even hear them breathing. The donkey, who had, in the meanwhile, went and slipped out the back door and sneaked around the house, was now waiting on the front porch all ready to go into action.

Wild Hair Willy didn't see anything in the shadows. He was a little bit hard of hearing and seeing anyways on account of his body filth. He walked on over to the fireplace to take a flint and strike it to get a fire going with the little bit of firewood and paper that he'd left in there earlier, but when Wild Hair Willy leaned down close to the fireplace it scared the poor old cat. She took her claws and fast as she could MERRROW! She reared up and commenced to scratching up his face and hands, MERRROW! MERRROW! MERRROW! she roared.

Jack and his friends managed to out-wit Wild Hair Willy, the worst
of the cut-throat robbers that there ever was.

Willy was so surprised that he shot straight up and bumped his head on the top of the fireplace. He was hollering and jumping around in pain. "Oh, my hurt head, don't cut me no more, don't cut me I says!" He was screaming and a-clutching at his face.

He was trying to get out the door; he didn't know what was attacking him in that darkness, but just as he made his way near the front door, the dog jumped out and chomped a hold of Willy's knee right good and firm with his big old teeth.

ARRG! Willy was a-screaming and a-hollering and running up and down the room in the darkness, yelling, "No, no, don't stab me no more! Don't stab me!" He was trying to get away and, finally, in the chaos he did manage to make his way out onto the front porch...

...just in time for the donkey to turn around and POW! Why, that old donkey, he mule-kicked that mean old Willy right on up high into the air. Willy was a-screaming and a-hollering the whole way up and the whole way right back down.

Willy fell down to the ground and made a loud CRASH! when he hit. He was scrambling to try to get up on his feet right away, and it was a good thing too because up there on the top of the roof was that old rooster just a waiting his turn to cause mischief, calling out, "KAW, KAW, KAW!"

Willy was so panic-stricken that he couldn't hear right. What he heard was what sounded like someone shouting, "Throw him up to me!" Wild Hair Willy took off running for his life.

When he got up to his band of robbers in the bushes, he said, "Come on boys, let's get a-moving, there is a whole gang that has taken over our house. They're fierce. They're terrible. Why the one in the fireplace had all these knives on him and those knives were so sharp... Why I just think we don't have a chance against him. Look at my pretty face, it's all ruined." He started to run and his robber gang ran with him.

Willy went on telling his cronies what had happened to him, "Then there was that other fella, the one with the hatchet, I don't haff to tell you how it was, why, just look at how he mangled up my pretty leg. I tell you it's all I can do to run for my life."

The robber gang was helping Wild Hair Willy along and they were running even faster. Willy was their boss, the biggest and the baddest of them. If he was scared, then they supposed that there was a good reason to be scared and that they should be too. Willy went on to tell his gang about the fella on the front porch wielding two sledgehammers that knocked him clean to Christmas. "We have got to get out of here, the one just a-sittin on the roof said 'throw him up to me, I'll tear him limb from limb.' ARG!"

Willy and the robbers scrambled up to their feet so fast and hard that they ran on down the road without looking back even once over their shoulder. To tell you the truth, they ran so fast and far that they ran clean right out of town. They ran so fast and far that they ran clear out of the county. They ran so fast and far that they ran clear out of the state of North Carolina. They ran so fast and far... It has been said that they were seen out in California and were still a-running. The last time anyone had ever seen them robbers they were running straight out into the Pacific Ocean.

Well, that was the end of Wild Hair Willy. There was much celebrating and patting on the back between Jack and his friends as they congratulated one another. Jack and the animals stayed there a few more days, as there was plenty of food for them all.

After that, the local sheriff stopped by the house because word of their good deed had spread. He said, "I want to shake your hand boy. You have single-handedly taken care of the scourge of the Carolinas. Wild Hair Willy has had a big old reward on his head for a long, long time now. Here you go, son."

To everyone's surprise the Sheriff of those parts handed Jack a big old sack of reward money. Oh boy, Jack and company were rich-folks now. Jack was so excited that he started making plans right away on how he was gonna spend it all.

A few days later, after the excitement of the great adventure had calmed down, Jack was sitting in the rocking chair feeling a bit blue. He said to his animal friends, "You know, this is nice and all, but I sure do miss my mamma."

"Aww," said the donkey. "We know you do, Jack, but we're all a family now and we have to stick together after everything we've been through. Besides, I don't know if your mamma would let all of us move in with you on the farm. You may not have enough room in that old barn of theirs for all of us."

Jack pondered on that a little bit as he rocked back and forth in the rocking chair thinking about his mamma and how much he really did miss her and the rest of his family back home. He finally said to his animal friends, "Well, we just got to go back to my old home and try. I'll give Mamma the gold anyway and then maybe we can figure something out after that."

It was then that Jack and the donkey, and the dog, and the cat, and the rooster all went on back down the road boggity-boggity, boggity-boggity, boggity-boggity,

boggity! As they came close to Jack's family home, they saw Mamma off in the distance. She had in her hands a handmade broom and was busy sweeping the porch and she was crying too—crying with big old tears running down her cheeks—but when Mamma saw Jack coming out of the clearing she dropped her broom and went on a-running over to him. Her apron was just a-flapping. She grabbed him up in the greatest, biggest hug of all time and kissed him all over.

Jack was so happy to have his mamma's arms around him... She just smelled so good. He was crying too.

She said, "Jack, don't ever run away again. We were all so worried about you. It's just not worth it, the heartache it caused, over a little bit of firewood. My poor precious son, where have you been all this time?"

She could tell her Jack was dirty, but he sure didn't look hungry. She was wondering what his story was.

"Well, "Jack said slowly, "Mamma, I made a few friends on my travels and they are here with me now. Honestly, we just can't bear to part company with one another after all we been through together. Do you think maybe we could have a few more folks added to our family?"

His mamma looked around and from the clearing came the donkey, dog, cat, and rooster. The group of them just stood there before her looking as pitiful as can be.

"Well, of course, we can take them in Jack," Mamma said. "There is always room for one more in our family."

Well, I'll tell you what—there was so much rejoicing and happiness when Jack told his parents and brothers and sisters the whole long story about how he and his new animal friends met up, how they together defeated Wild Hair Willy and earned for themselves a big bag of gold as a reward—and because of the brave actions of Jack and the animals, from that day on the family didn't have to worry about food or firewood or expenses ever again.

And each night, as he laid his weary head down to sleep upon his pillow, Jack reminded himself just how thankful he was to be back home among his beloved family. He was also so happy to have his mamma's home cooking once again too. Jack always remembered, even when he was an old grand-daddy, that having a family that loves you is a far, far better thing to have than all the gold that the world has to offer.

Grandma Mary Brown's Corn Pudding

Ingredients

- 4 eggs, slightly beaten
- 1 tablespoon of flour
- 2 cups of milk
- 1 teaspoon salt
- 1/2 cup of sugar
- 1 stick of melted butter
- 2 cups of kernel corn, off the cob

Directions

Preheat oven to 350 Fahrenheit

Beat the eggs with milk and sugar first, and then add all the other ingredients

Pour the mixture into a 9" square pan

Bake 1 hour or until lightly browned on top

Serve warm

Notes from Cyn:

Jack and the robbers is an old-time "Jack" story and they have been collected and told and retold over the years. They were collected by Richard Chase, who, as some of you may know, was a folk lore collector. He literally went from house to house, porch to porch up in the mountains of North Carolina, talking to folks and hearing their stories as they told them. Then, he wrote them all down in a book called *The Jack Tales*, which was published in the 1920s and in another book he called *Grandfather Tales: American-English Folk Tales*, published in 1948.

We sometimes forget that back then there were not restaurants or fast-food restaurants on every corner. Cooking at home was an arduous job because much of the food was cooked in the fireplace. Everything eaten by the family was grown on the land, raised in the fields, or traded for with goods from other nearby families. As we've talked about before, with no television, computers, DVDs, or telephones getting in the way, family storytelling was an important part of family time and entertainment. This was especially true at meals and afterward.

Mommy Jewel's Chocolate Pound Cake

Ingredients:

8 ounces (2 sticks) butter, softened

1 to 2 teaspoons pure vanilla extract

8 ounces sour cream

1 teaspoon almond extract

2-1/4 cups cake flour

1 teaspoon baking powder

3 cups sugar

3/4 cup rich cocoa powder

6 eggs

Directions:

Preheat the oven to 325 degrees F. Grease and flour a 10-inch Bundt pan

Using an electric mixer, cream together the butter, sour cream, and sugar

Add the eggs, 2 at a time, beating well after each addition

Add the vanilla and almond extracts

In another bowl, stir together the flour, baking powder, and cocoa

Add 1/2 the flour mixture to the creamed mixture, beat well, add the remaining 1/2
flour mixture, and continue to beat at medium speed for 2 minutes

Pour the batter into the prepared pan and bake for 1 hour 15 minutes

Continue to bake for an additional 15 minutes if necessary, but do not open the oven
to check the cake for at least 1 hour

Notes from Cyn:

Pound cake is a family favorite down here in the South. Many of my friends make it. Our church cook books from the 1980s and 1990s usually had one or two different recipes for pound cake. Most recipes for it are about the same. If you want a plain pound cake flavored with only vanilla or almond flavor you can use my recipe without adding the cocoa. Either way you make it, this cake is moist and good to the last crumb but this recipe, with the chocolate in it, is the one that I make most often!

Mommy Jewel, my husband Fred's grandmother, was famous for her pound cake. After she passed away, I was the one who inherited her precious pound cake pan. The many memories a mere baking pan can bring back is incredible. Mommy Jewel made a pound cake for all special occasions as well as for birthday presents. She did this even after she was older and sick with cancer. We miss them today, those pound cakes of hers, but luckily we have the pan, the story, and the memories that go along with them.

16 | HOW MEAT LOVES SALT

This Traditional Folktale comes with a Recipe for Fred's Ole Timey Bone Suckin Pork Ribs

Once upon a time there was a very wealthy king who had four very beautiful daughters. One-by-one they were courted by handsome princes from foreign lands... One-by-one they became engaged... One-by-one they were married to their prince and went on to live happily ever after. All except, that is, for the king's fourth and youngest daughter. He had always thought to himself that she was plain and not as smart as her older sisters because she was not beautiful. In fact, everyone said that about her and treated her as such—plain and simple—but this treatment of her frustrated the king so because she was the sweetest girl and had the nicest personality of any one he had ever met. He enjoyed spending time with her and every night they always sat down together in the great dining hall and ate dinner together.

As the king grew older, he began preparing the kingdom for his eventual death by choosing an heir to the throne. Since he had no sons to pass his crown on to, the king decided that he would leave his entire kingdom and all his wealth to the daughter who loved him the most because in his mind it meant that she would also be the one who loved the land as much as he did and would do the best job of ruling the people after he was gone. How was he to decide this, though? What sort of test could he give them?

One day the king decided that the daughter who was the best cook and prepared for him the best and most delicious meal would be the one who loved him the most and thereby named the winner of the contest and the heir to the kingdom.

Well, of course, the daughters who were already married were not only great chefs in their own right, but had huge kitchens in their palace homes and a huge cooking staff of trained chefs to assist them. The plain and unmarried youngest daughter... Well, she could not cook very well at all, but each night at dinner she sat at the end of the dining room table and she and her father would eat there together. She would watch him take his meals, eating his meat and vegetables, but before he took a single bite of anything on his plate, he'd put lots and lots of salt on it.

Now you have to remember that back then, centuries and centuries ago, salt was such a prized commodity that it was used as currency in some places. In fact, centuries ago a small local war was fought over the salt trade in Germany. The war ended with the burning of the bridge in Frisen, a little monastery town. Fortunately, it managed to go on to survive as a small and sleepy little village, but, unfortunately, because it lost the skirmish to Munich, it did not go on to become the capitol of Bavaria.

Salt was very important, as you can see, and the king, being a very wealthy man, had a lot of it.

The daughters, all four of them, each began to prepare their meals. The first one prepared the most wonderful feast he had ever eaten. The second one prepared an even better feast. The third one had a feast even better than the previous two. The king was just about to decide which one of his three daughters loved him the most as shown by their cooking when his fourth and youngest daughter asked if should could have her chance to prove her love for him. Couldn't she too please make him something to eat?

Sighing heavily, because he had just eaten three grand feasts, the king agreed.

When she brought her meal out and presented it to her father, the king, it was the plainest and most nondescript meal you could ever imagine being put on a plate. She set it down in front of her father, the king. She could see and hear her sisters and their husbands and their grand entourages laughing at her behind her back, but she didn't pay them any mind.

The father looked down at his plate of plain old food and gave a deep sigh wondering to himself just how good it could honestly be, but being a good king, as well as a good father, he decided that it was only fair that he taste what his youngest daughter had made for him. He took a taste and, to his great surprise, it was pretty good. Shocked by this discovery, he took another taste—and that one was even better. Soon he was eating up everything on his plate. He had eaten it down to the last crumb even though he was not the least bit hungry because he had just eaten three other feasts.

It's often said that food is the way to a man's heart. In the case it was
food with a whole lot of salt that won over this father, the king.

The king said, "Well, my youngest daughter, I truly think that you are going to be the winner." He smiled at her as he spoke because the king finally knew and understood. "Yes, my dear, you are the winner because you must truly, truly love me the most to know how to make a meat and vegetable dish with so much salt. To have done this means that of all my daughters, you alone are the only one who truly knows what it is that I like. You listened to me and learned. That will make you a good leader to our people. I freely give my crown and kingdom to you."

With that, the youngest daughter blossomed and inherited her father's wealth. She learned a great deal on leadership from him before he was gone, as she was determined to be a great ruler in her own right, and at every meal when they sat down together to eat, her father the king would turn to her and say to her with a smile, "I love you like meat loves salt."

Fred's Ole Timey Bone Sucking Pork Ribs

Ingredients:

1 onion, chopped

1 green pepper, chopped

garlic, salt, and pepper to taste

2 cans cheap beer (If you like a nonalcoholic version of this recipe then just use 2 cups of apple cider instead)

1-2 medium size country style cut pork ribs per person

Directions:

Pre-heat oven to 400 degrees Fahrenheit

Put ribs in a large roasting pan

Pour beer over them then add all the other things, except the sauce (see recipe on next page)

Put them in the oven and roast for 1/2 hour

Then turn the temperature down to 300 degrees and roast the ribs for 1 hour

Pour sauce generously over the ribs and cook another 1/2 hour

Add more sauce if desired and serve amid lots of compliments and yummy noises

If you want to grill them, pre-heat the grill and cook the ribs slowly, turning them often. They will get brown and crusty that way, but be careful as it's easy to catch ribs on fire! Baste them with the barbecue sauce and then cook on low for five minutes more on each side. The time will depend on the grill and the person whose doing the grilling... Just test them before you serve them up.

Barbecue Sauce Recipe

Ingredients:

2 cups tomato sauce
1 small onion, minced
3 tablespoons of minced garlic
1/2 cup of herb vinegar
1/2 cup of balsamic vinegar
1 or 2 teaspoons of hot sauce
1 small green pepper, chopped
Salt and pepper to taste
1 tablespoon of mustard

Directions:

Mix everything together and simmer slowly till it thickens
Remove from the heat and spoon on meat
You can easily double this if you want to
As Grandma Mary used to say, it's also "delish" on baked or grilled chicken
Use this sauce when needed; it'll keep up to two weeks in the refrigerator

Notes from Cyn:

This story began with the familiar "once upon a time" because some of the stories told up in the mountains of North Carolina were brought over to America from their original countries. Back in their old countries is where they had kings and queens and princes and princesses. When the stories were retold here, they left in all the old nobility, so even though we do not have kings and queens here in America, many of our old folktales do.

These pork ribs are a real crowd pleaser. You can bake them in the oven or cook them on the grill. They even go good with a lot of the other recipes we've been making, like the corn pudding and the potatoes... Well, you get the idea!

17 | OLE DRY FRY

A Tale with a Recipe for Chicken and Dumplings and Fried Green Tomatoes

Back in them good old days sometimes there wasn't even a preacher for every little town and farm on the mountain. In fact some places only had a traveling preacher and that's exactly what old Dry Fry was, a traveling preacher. He would be a-riding over to one settlement and preaching there one Sunday and then he would be a-riding on over to another place and preaching there on another Sunday and then he'd travel on to another community after that... and then onto another... and another.

It was customary, as there wasn't much money back in those days, to pay the preacher with a great big old Sunday supper as well as a small part of the offering from the church. Of course, the family who made the supper got to see the preacher the most. It was considered quite an honor to be the family to host the preacher.

Now as it happened there was this one preacher by the name of Old Dry Fry, and he loved chicken and dumplings and fried green tomatoes so much that they had it at every meal that he was invited to. He had chicken and dumplings and fried green tomatoes at Mrs. Smith's house and then he'd go over to the Henderson's farm and have chicken and dumplings and fried green tomatoes there as well. Of course he'd make sure that, when he went down the road a piece, to have chicken and dumplings and fried green tomatoes at the Jones' mill. It was about all the man ever ate.

Old Dry Fry would go to the Smith's house most often because he loved her chicken and dumplings and fried green tomatoes the best. It was said that he would do anything to get his hands on a plate of her food. One time it was said that when a slice of fried green tomato fell in a mud puddle that old Dry Fry went on after it. He beat the dogs to it, wiped it off just a bit, and gobbled it on up. He was that crazy for Mrs. Smith's fried green tomatoes.

Now one day Farmer Cobb had old Dry Fry over for a Sunday meeting dinner. They had chicken, of course, 'cause everybody knew that was Old Dry Fry's favorite. He loved Mrs. Cobb's chicken and dumplings too so she made sure she had made a whole mess of it.

When dinner time came old Dry Fry sat himself down at the table and fixed himself a big old plate of food and he began sucking down chicken and dumplings as fast as he could. It was said that the preacher could eat a whole chicken in just about five minutes. He was sucking all that food down so fast that all of a sudden ACH! ARG! GASP! a bone got stuck in his throat. He was gasping and coughing and having such a time breathing that right before the family's very eyes old Dry Fry turned blue and collapsed THUNK! dead on the supper table. It all happened so fast that there wasn't anything anyone could have done to save him.

"Oh no!" they screamed as everybody was going crazy. "Oh no! What are we gonna do? Why, folks are gonna think that we killed old Dry Fry!"

"They're gonna put us in jail!" exclaimed Aunt Lucy in a panic. "They'll hang us by our scrawny necks. They'll think that we killed old Dry Fry on purpose. What are we gonna do?"

Well, the family gathered up together and stewed and talked about it all day long. It was just pure mayhem in that old mountain farmhouse. Ole Dry Fry just sat there sprawled out on the ruined supper table, dead as a doornail.

Finally, come the end of the day, right toward dark, one of the family members had an idea. It was Cousin Arleen and she said, "Why don't we just put old Dry Fry in a gunnysack and leave him there on the side of the road? They'll just think he's some trash and someone will eventually pick it up and toss it down into the holler. Nobody will know the truth of what happened."

So that's just what they did.

Daddy and the boys got a great big gunnysack and put old Dry Fry into it. They toted it down over to the holler in the dead of night and, when nobody was looking, that gunnysack with old Dry Fry in it went thunk, thunk, thunk, thunk, thunk as it went a-rolling on down the hill.

Now, unbeknownst to the Cobb boys, at the bottom of the hill were two brothers, Jeb and Ted. They were so dumb those two boys. Now, I know it's not nice to talk about folks who have no smartness about them, but Jeb and Ted were so dumb they believed that if you stood out in the rain with your mouth opened, you could drown.

So, as they were sitting there on a log doing nothing in the middle of the night, Jeb and Ted saw this gunnysack coming down the hill thunk, thunk, thunk, thunk, thunk.

"Oh, my gosh!" they shouted as they jumped up in excitement. "We got something wonderful now. Why, I just bet that somebody threw out a whole sack full of potatoes. We could sell it and make a lot of money. Mamma will be so proud of us."

Jeb and Ted went over to the gunnysack, cut it open, and saw what was inside AAHH! There before them lying as dead as a doornail was old Dry Fry. The boys took one look at him and they screeched in shock. They knew who he was. Everybody knew who he was—and here he was, dead.

"Oh, Lawda Mercy," said Jeb, "That's the preacher, old Dry Fry. If we say anything to anybody bout this, they gonna think it was us who killed him. They'll put us in the jail and hang us high. We got to do something."

Jeb and Ted got to thinking and between them they finally came up with an idea. They went and put old Dry Fry back in the gunnysack and then they carried it, sneaking up and over, to the Jones' smokehouse.

Now, back in those days, you didn't have refrigerators and you didn't have stores where you went and bought your meat. No sir, you smoked it yourself with a low burning fire as it hung there up in the smokehouse. Usually this was done with big old ham hocks and usually they still had the burlap sack still on them when they got hung up there. The sack would get taken off as the ham was more and more cured or smoked that is.

Jeb and Ted hung old Dry Fry in the Jones' smokehouse figuring it would be a long while before anybody got to that sack. They hung it up next to the biggest and juiciest ham they could find and then they backed out and closed the door really quietly, so as not to wake the house as the family slept.

Old Dry Fry loved chicken and dumplings and fried green tomatoes so much that they were the end of him.

The next morning farmer Jones' wife went out to the smokehouse. Custom was that you left your meat out there until you got ready to cook it for breakfast. You'd go out there and slice off as much meat as you needed for the meal and leave the rest. Sometimes you'd cut off some bacon for breakfast. Sometimes you'd cut off a big chunk of meat to roast for dinner. Other times you cut off some fatback for frying. It just depended on what and how much you needed, so Mrs. Jones went out to the smokehouse and opened up a sack of meat meaning to cut some bacon off to make for her family for breakfast. Instead, out fell old Dry Fry—right at her feet!

AHH! She screamed murder loud and long jumping up and down the whole while. Her husband came running over, her children came running over, and still she screamed and screamed. When her whole family got to where she was, they stopped and looked at what she was screaming about. "Oh, my gosh!" they said in shock and disbelief. "Why, it's old Dry Fry."

"Oh no," cried Mrs. Jones, "what are we gonna do? They are gonna come and put me in jail and hang me dead. They may even take the farm. What will y'all do?" She was beside herself with grief and terror.

It was broad daylight and Mr. Jones knew that he had to do something fast, so he said to his wife, "Now don't you go on worrying like that. I have got this taken care of. I have an idea; you get the children and go on up to the house."

So that's what she did.

Now farmer Jones had an old mule he didn't use much for anything anymore. It had been out to pasture for a long time and he figured that everyone around these parts had just about forgotten that he even had it anymore, so farmer Jones went and got his old mule and took it over to where poor old Dry Fry lay. He took up the dead preacher and propped him atop the mule and then, using some rope, he carefully tied old Dry Fry's hands to the mule's neck so it looked like he was hanging on tight. He used some more rope and tied old Dry Fry's feet down to the side of the mule so it looked like he was riding him. Next, he led that old mule down to the main road that went straight by and through the town. Finally, farmer Jones faced the mule in the right direction and WACK! gave it a slap on its old rump so hard that it set that mule to running.

BAM! That mule took off as fast as it ever could have. Like a streak of lightning, it shot down the road and the way the preacher man was tied on up there it looked like old Dry Fry was racing that mule as hard as it could go. The mule ran and ran and old Dry Fry was just a-bopping and a-bopping up and down tied on as he was.

That mule ran past every house and ran through many a fence. It never stopped and, as it ran, folks who saw it pass on by said, "Why, there goes old Dry Fry. What's he is such a hurry for?"

That mule ran so fast and so hard it ran right on out of the town and right on out of the county. Some folks in Kentucky saw him, another bunch in Arizona too. Everyone who saw him wiz on by said, "Why, there goes old Dry Fry!" Guess that mule just kept a-runnin' all the way to California because that preacher was never seen in these parts again and, you know, between you and me, I don't think that the folks in that area ever did figure out that old Dry Fry had died and wasn't just out riding out around the countryside. They sure did miss him and his preaching though, but there was not one single wife that missed having to cook all those chicken and dumplings and fried green tomatoes because he sure could eat a lot for such a skinny man.

Grandma Moore's Chicken Pot Pie

Ingredients:

- 1 three or more pound chicken cut into pieces
- 2 or 3 ribs of celery, chopped
- 1 large onion, chopped

Directions:

- Place the chicken, celery, and onion, in a large pot
- Add enough water to cover the chicken
- Bring to a simmer over medium heat
- Simmer the chicken until it is tender, about 20 to 30 minutes
- Remove the chicken and debone the pieces
- Return the chicken to the pot and keep warm

Dumplings

Ingredients

- 2 cups of all-purpose flour
- 1 teaspoon of salt
- About 3/4 cup of ice water

Directions:

- Mix the flour and the salt together
- Mound in a mixing bowl
- At the center of the mound, make a well and add small amounts of ice water gradually and mix with your hands
- Knead the dough and form it into a ball.
- Put some flour on a counter or other clean, flat surface
- Roll out the dough to about 1/4 inch in thickness
- Allow the dough to rest
- Cut the dough into 2-inch pieces about 4 or 5 inches long
- Drop one by one into the simmering soup
- Cook until the dumplings float and are no longer doughy, 3 to 4 minutes
- Do not stir very much after this point as this will break up the dumplings
- Serve in bowls immediately

For a modern twist, you can add a can of cream of chicken or cream of mushroom soup to the broth right before the raw dumplings are added. Additional herbs can be added if you like, such as a tablespoon of garlic, a tablespoon of rosemary, a tablespoon of thyme, and a tablespoon of sweet basil.

Notes from Cyn:

The life of an itinerate minister was a hard one. If they were lucky enough to have one, they rode a horse or mule from parish to parish and church to church. At each stop along the way they would have to stay with families and eat what the family was having. There were no hotels to stay in or diners to eat at. Back then the sharing of room and board was considered partial payment for his services as well as a gift of "caring" from each family. Another good example of home cookin' elevated to an importance in this way and others.

Fresh herbs are easy to grow in a sunny window box inside your home during the winter and pots outside in full sun during the spring, summer, and fall seasons. Try not to over water. Several herbs, such as Rosemary and mint may last through the winter outside in a sheltered place, but only if they are grown in the ground.

Fried Green Tomatoes

(Makes 4 Servings)

Ingredients:

6 large green tomatoes (about 3 pounds)
2 tablespoons of lemon juice (or a few dashes of hot sauce)
1/2 cup of cornmeal
2 teaspoons of freshly ground black pepper
Nonstick cooking spray

Directions:

Slice each tomato into 1/2 inch thick slices
Sprinkle the lemon juice or hot sauce on the tomatoes
Mix the cornmeal and black pepper in a plastic bag
Put tomato slices into the bag and shake well
Coat a cast-iron skillet or nonstick sauté pan with nonstick cooking spray
Fry the tomatoes, over medium-high heat, until they are light brown on each side
A few dashes of Louisiana Hot Sauce can be used instead of lemon juice to give these
    fried green tomatoes a spicier flavor.

Notes from Cyn:

I have a dear friend who is allergic to red tomatoes but for some reason he can eat green tomatoes. He and his wife have created several recipes using green tomatoes instead of the red ripened ones. His "Bloody Mary Cocktails" and "Stewed Tomatoes" are unique looking to say the least. They taste very different, but that's the great thing about cooking—you can do it your way.

Afterword

"Just a little more . . ."

There you have it—a small snack and a little bit of Southern folktales mixed in with some old and new recipes. Guess I will get a little preaching in too.

Medical research has taught us that a low-fat, low calorie, low sugar, and moderate eating diet is essential for a healthy body. I am not advocating throwing that out the window so we can return to tables piled high with fat, carbohydrates, and too much salt. I just want to have a comforting respite, a moment now and then to experience the warmth and feeling of time honored traditions and recipes.

I have had eating issues my whole life. I could write a jumbo "how-to-book" for weight loss. Then I could write one on "how-not-to" as well. Yes, I admit, I am obsessed with food, but this time I feel empowered by food because the result of my obsession has been this collection.

That said, I also want to share some tips for making the old recipes healthier. I try to cook most of these recipes revised with less salt, sugar, and healthier oils. Meats baked and grilled, not fried, with extra herbs and seasonings are a healthy substitute. I recommend using whole grain flour and low or nonfat substitutes. Yes, I know, they don't taste exactly the same but they are so similar and good enough that you get used to them. There are many other healthful tips if you don't mind being a little creative, such as like using honey or fruit juice in place of processed white granulated sugar.

The important point here, though, is to enjoy the sharing aspect of cooking all the while keeping to the family tradition.

I have seen a change evolving in recent years. With the wars, uncertain finances, and overall upheaval everywhere, these certainly are troubled times we live in. People want things like they used to be and are turning back to the comfort of the long familiar. Cooking and eating food the way it used to be, food from our childhood and happier times, it makes us feel safe, loved, and protected. This sort of nostalgia can also bring soothing closeness with friends and family or rekindle relationships that have begun to unravel. The hard economic times of this current era have necessitated less restaurant meals eaten out and more at home cooking. The advent of all the cooking shows and celebrity chefs has helped foster the idea that cooking now is not only utilitarian and cost effective but also that it can be a lot of family-time fun. So please have a good time with all the folk tales I've chosen to include in this book and by all means, please do enjoy the home cookin!!

Recipes Index